In The Carpenter's Workshop

Volume 2

An Exploration Of The Use Of Drama In Story Sermons

Jerry Eckert

CSS Publishing Company, Inc., Lima, Ohio

Copyright © 1997 by
CSS Publishing Company, Inc.
Lima, Ohio

Some scripture quotations are from the *Revised Standard Version of the Bible*, copyrighted 1946, 1952 ©, 1971, 1973, by the Division of Christian Education of the National Council of the Churches of Christ in the USA. Used by permission.

Some scripture quotations are from the *Good News Bible,* in Today's English Version. Copyright © American Bible Society 1966, 1971, 1976. Used by permission.

Library of Congress Cataloging-in-Publication Data

Eckert, Jerry O., 1935-
   In the Carpenter's workshop : an exploration of the use of drama in story sermons / Jerry O. Eckert.
     p.   cm.
   ISBN 0-7880-0760-2
   1. Story sermons. 2 Methodist Church — Sermons. 3. Sermons, American. I. Title.
BV4307.S7E34   1997
252—dc20   96-38672
                                                    CIP

This book is available in the following formats, listed by ISBN:
    0-7880-0761-0   Book
    0-7880-1045-X   Mac
    0-7880-1046-8   IBM 3 1/2
    0-7880-1194-4   Sermon Prep

PRINTED IN U.S.A.

I'm dedicating this book to those in our churches who trigger our imaginations. Let me identify two.

Marshall Bruch is an active member of Faith Players, the group that inspired me to try a variety of formats for my preaching. He was (and still is) six feet tall, weighs around 240 pounds, and has black shaggy hair and beard. He looks so much like John the Baptist must have looked that he became John the Baptist in an interview I wrote. I could hear him saying the words I wrote down. He performed "God, the Son" with me with only a few minutes to review the text.

My daughter Karen was a product of her environment. The way she talked was so characteristic that again I enjoyed the privilege of hearing her in my inner ear as I wrote the interview in "The Man Born Blind." "Do I really talk this way?" she asked as she was looking at the text on the way to church. She did because she flowed through it like it was made for her.

To have such laity in our churches gives us opportunities to approach some texts in ways we would never consider using the monologue-style sermon.

To these folks is this second volume dedicated.

Acknowledgments

Becoming a published author has been a learning experience, mainly learning two things: appreciation for work done by the publisher's staff and then discovering what else is going on in the world of worship and drama.

I owe thanks to Tom Lentz, who accepted my manuscript; Teresa Rhoads, who edited and guided the text through publication; and Sherry Neuenschwander, who has helped with the marketing. Thanks to all the others at CSS Publishing Company who have had anything to do with getting these little volumes out. They have been most generous of their time and attention in guiding me through the process.

Sherry was assigned to help me do book signings, get radio and newspaper interviews, and be liaison with CSS to anyone I knew who might be interested in the significance of my book. She has opened doors to a world I could never have seen without her help. At every single book signing, whether in Syracuse or Shreveport, Philadelphia or Milwaukee, I have met wonderfully creative people doing imaginative things in their ministries. What pleased me was that they took my book as support and encouragement to do what they are doing. So far, it appears there is a national interest in using storytelling and drama in worship, in Sunday school, in evangelism, in youth work, in providing chaplaincy, and in outreach to the functionally illiterate. I never would have had a chance to see the scope had it not been for Sherry working so hard to get me into "public relations" kinds of activities. I dreaded having to "sell" my book. Now it is a delight because it puts me in touch with so many gifted Christians, and I look forward to the next opportunity Sherry sets up because I know I'll meet more!

A special thanks to Pastor Wesley T. Runk who "runs" CSS, who had a vision to see something in my work that I didn't dream.

Jerry Eckert

P.S. I also owe my brother, Jack A. Eckert, a great deal for his assistance on the computer. More on his work in Volume 3.

TAblE Of CONTENTS

Foreword

I am often asked what it is like to prepare a sermon. Most preachers struggle because we don't like to do the same themes over and over again. We, too, want to expand our search of the scriptures to find God's Word for today. What often gets us going is a question a church member asks or a situation which requires the response of the church. Even if we start with the lectionary, the passage among the set that gives our minds direction and our souls a chance to express themselves is the one that says something about what our church folks (and we ourselves) are up against in life.

When it comes to writing these drama sermons, however, a kind of creativity can engulf us and something flows in ways that surprise us. I spent extra hours looking for historical details and facts out of the life of the culture of Bible times. I usually had a sense of direction with what I was wanting to do. Once I had enough detail to fill in around the story told in the Bible, I then had to pick a genre, a format that would share the story the best. Then I would just start writing. It helps to have a computer word processor!

Of course, I had to review and revise. And sometimes I had to hit the books again for more detail or to resolve a question I hadn't thought to research. But all of us do that same thing anyway, sometimes on the way to our second church or between services!

The most stunning experience I had was the writing of the sermon, "The Adventure Of The Empty Tomb." As I say in the comment at the beginning of that sermon, I heard Dr. Watson dictating the story. I literally had no idea how it was going to come out! I couldn't wait to finish it to see how it ended.

Most of the time I put myself into the place of the person from whose point of view the story was told, and tried to see it through his/her eyes. I did not always hear that person's voice but it became my task to press the Bible and the commentaries and Bible

7

dictionaries until I could see more clearly what I could do and where that led.

I hope you sense the fun I had working with the materials and formats because I anticipate others being far more creative and effective doing this. I long to see you sense the joy of preaching that comes out of varying your voice(s) and presentation.

But the preacher and teacher are not my only concern.

In seminary, I was taught that the best sermons were what goes on in the heads of the congregation as they are listening rather than what we preachers have to say. Triggering that internal dialogue and imagination is the perennial task of the pastor. But so is helping them to understand and not challenging them all the time.

What I hope to achieve by this sharing is to further the variety of ways sermons may be constructed and to include our talented laity in the proclamation in another way. Please do not presume that this is the last word in proclamation. Please do not restrict your imaginations about involving church members to what is found here.

My hope is that these three little books further open the window and let in some more fresh air.

Introduction

"You will find the imperative in the indicative." That was one of the principal ways Dr. Scubert Ogden handled ethics. I thought I understood what he was teaching us at the time (1962).

The impression I had was that rather than systematizing ethical thought, Dr. Ogden was urging us to let what was happening in itself call forth our moral responsibilities. "Situation ethics" was being written about and may have been part of my understanding at the time. So rather than bringing a latticework of ethical directions to bear on a circumstance, such as whether divorce was right or wrong, it seems he was asking us to look carefully at the situation and decide what was the most loving response to that situation.

I asked him how we were supposed to love the rabbits that were eating the newly-sprouted wheat which was being grown to provide bread for the community. As such classroom exchanges go sometimes, the answer was not exactly thoroughly explained, but I recall he said, "Shoot them with love!"

In effect, we face the possibility of having to break a law of God to fulfill another law of God. But that illustrated the ethical dilemma of life. Our choices are not always between good and bad, right and wrong. They are often between two goods or two bads. Worse, they often involve conflicting ethical directions. Jesus had hungry disciples, but the law said they couldn't harvest any grains. A man born blind asked Jesus' help on the Sabbath, but to heal the man was a violation of the Sabbath laws. Jesus taught then that we were not made for the Sabbath but the Sabbath for us. That in turn has become a new law to the point where there no longer is a Sabbath for most people. We end up working seven days a week. Which is the right thing to do? Be in the saddle nonstop because we are needed, or break off on a regular basis to rest those sore nerves? Going back to the dilemma over the possibility of stripping a few grains of wheat to assuage hunger pangs on the Sabbath, do we feed the hungry or do we honor God?

Actually, I don't think Dr. Ogden was taking us into "situational ethics" at all, though at the time, it was hard not to slip over into that kind of thinking.

I now believe what he was doing was to get us to live in a situation and see the inherent moral issues in those events. You are a father who is widowed. You live just above poverty. You are in a culture which treats women and children as things and which obligates you to go on pilgrimage. What do you do with your infant daughter? Or many years ago, you were done a great wrong by your brothers. And now, not realizing you are still alive nor recognizing you, they come to you for help. You have the perfect opportunity to stick it to them. Or you are constantly being harassed by those who believe very differently about religion. And your best friend now calls you to try to calm you down so you can see the point of your harassers and maybe move on to reconciliation.

These are not exactly the moral dilemmas everyone faces, but they illustrate some of the things that can happen to you or me. You will see the dramatized story sermon becomes a means to examine the moral issues without becoming preachy. Rather than setting down orderly guidelines, we use the story to draw the listener into looking at the moral imperative from the inside instead of from the outside.

Perhaps it is time for a revival of the morality plays of the Middle Ages. In truth, we may already have something like that going on in our culture now. Only the contemporary "morality plays" are romance novels. Probably the most popular and widely experienced genres of our day are the romance novels. LaVerle Spencer and Judith McNaught have probably had more influence over folks than the Pope and all the preachers combined simply because they tell riveting stories in which ethical dilemmas are lived by vivid and plausible folks. McNaught's *Whitney, My Love* does as much to undercut arrogance as John 13 and Spencer's *Twice Loved* explores the nature of love in ways that make John 15:15 more understandable.

Other contemporary writing that has moved people includes *To Kill A Mockingbird*, the first section of Viktor Frankl's *Man's Search for Meaning* where he speaks of his experiences surviving a concentration camp, *The Autobiography of Malcolm X*, and John Hersey's *Hiroshima.*

And don't we worry about television's impact on our morality? Don't we cherish a program like *The Commish* which illustrated how nonviolent means can often be used to resolve potentially violent situations?

Maybe we need to deepen our understanding of the power of stories to get across our message in a milieu where other story tellers are having such profound impact, not always for the good.

Maybe that's what Dr. Ogden meant. Obviously we need to explore the indicative in order to demonstrate the imperative. And sometimes the indicative forces us to reevaluate our imperatives.

Maybe that's the real urgency calling upon us to try more than monologues in our preaching.

Comment: I have always wondered how Jesus gathered his Disciples. The way the biblical stories go, it seems like he knew most of them one way or another. So I hypothesized that they may have known each other as children. How, since they were from a number of different towns not that close together, could they have had contact?

Having taught a few lab schools, I decided that maybe something like that might have occurred! Since the Sunday for which I was preparing was Rally Day, I wondered what a teacher giving a report on such a lab school would say. What do you think s/he would say?

Jesus And The Disciples
Mark 10:23-31

I thank you for this chance to describe the lab school we attended at Chorazin last month.

A lab school is a training session for synagogue teachers. Not all teachers at synagogue are rabbis. So the Council of Rabbis set up this workshop to train the lay teachers. Children came from as far away as Nazareth to the southwest, Caesarea Philippi to the north, and as far south as Kerioth.

The children who attended were fairly wealthy, with a few exceptions, and bright. The richest one came from way down in Kerioth, south of Jerusalem. His name was Judas. The synagogues in the area, Cana, Bethsaida, Capernaum, Magdala, all sent kids, too.

There were three boys from Nazareth who were not so well off. They were teased because no one expects anything good to come out of Nazareth. Their mother came along. She was very nice. Her name was Mary. We got to be good friends.

She and I watched the eight- to twelve-year-old class that a Rabbi Gamaliel taught in the mornings.

It was interesting how the children grouped up. There were three who were shy. Mary's two younger boys, James and Jude, were joined by the little boy from Kerioth. He rode down with Rabbi but was about the quietest one there. Then there were the bright ones who were really ready to speak up: Levi, Bartholomew, Mary, and Jesus, my friend's oldest boy. Then there were the jocks: Peter, Thomas, Simon, Andrew, and Philip. At least they enjoyed the long-muscle activities more than the others. And we had our share of goof-offs, James and John. Mary took responsibility for trying to keep them in line. Their father had paid for her and her boys to come to the lab school, so she felt obligated to keep those two in tow.

The first day, the Rabbi worked to get them all acquainted with each other. They all gave their names, where they were from, and how old they were. They were asked to tell their favorite story from Genesis. James and John disappeared right in the middle of Levi's telling the creation story. Mary found them in the Moses chair next to the Scroll cabinet.

The little girl from Magdala, Mary is also her name, was right there with her favorite story, about the snake in the garden of Eden. Some of the others were a lot less confident, but pretty soon, everybody had told a story and it looked like the Rabbi was going to do all right.

In the afternoon, we went down to the Sea of Galilee to swim and relax. The two of us women would not have been able to keep track of them if it had not been for Philip and Andrew. They volunteered to be "life guards." Being twelve and about to do their bar mitzvahs, they were ready to act grown up.

They organized a race. Only Bartholomew stayed in the shallows. He couldn't swim. Judas could and so could the little girl. Andrew started them off and Philip stood at the finish line.

It was a good race. But the winner was a surprise. It wasn't Peter or Simon, the two biggest boys. It was Mary. She is not big, but she went through the water like a fish and won easily.

If you wonder why I tell this story, which is not about the lab school session, it is because of what happened the next morning in class.

Rabbi Gamaliel asked them about what happened at the lake. Simon got up and said girls shouldn't be allowed at lab school. Rabbi turned to the class and asked them what they thought.

At first, no one said anything. Simon is a strong kid so those who disagreed with him could be in trouble. But it looked like everyone agreed with him. My friend and I looked at each other, feeling very bad. Then Jesus raised his hand.

"May I ask Simon some questions?" he offered. The Rabbi nodded.

"Simon, who made you?"

Simon looked at Jesus as though he were asking a dumb question. "God did," he said curtly.

Jesus asked his second question. "Who made Mary?"

Simon knew he was loser again when he said, "God did."

Rabbi added, "Enough said!"

From that point on, that group was welded together. Oh, they goofed off and they fussed over things, but they did everything together. It became quite a close bunch.

On the last day, they were finishing their work on the Ten Commandments.

Rabbi went around the circle. "Is there anyone here who can be obedient to God?"

All the children jumped up saying they could be obedient.

"Are you sure?"

"Yes, yes!" they all said.

"How?"

"By obeying God's laws," they said as if they were one voice.

"Such as?"

"Honor your parents," one said. "Thou shalt not steal," another said. "Thou shalt not kill," said a third.

"How can you honor your parents?" Rabbi asked.

As the others answered the questions, Rabbi calmly walked over to the Moses chair and plucked James and John out of it. Mary hadn't seen them slip off.

"But what if your parents are wrong?" asked Thomas.

"They're still your parents," answered Bartholomew.

"But what if they ask you to do something wrong?" Philip asked.

"Yes, what if your parents asked you to go and beg?" Rabbi brought in.

The kids all laughed. "No, we work hard. When you work hard, there is no need to beg," Levi said.

Not even Thomas challenged that.

Peter and Simon were talking about going swimming. James and John were looking for a way to sneak out again. Mary was looking at Jesus. Everyone else was quiet. They couldn't imagine being poor enough to have your parents ask such a crazy thing.

Jesus wasn't still, however. He pulled an upholstering needle out of his shirt. He took a piece of string out of his pocket and tied some "camels" (knots) in it. He tried to put the knotted string through the needle's eye, and, of course it wouldn't go.

Rabbi picked up on it right away. He said, "It is harder for the rich to be obedient to God than for a knot to go through the eye of a needle." He smiled at Jesus.

The other kids didn't seem to know what was going on. Mary and I were proud of Jesus' insight.

"You children are well off and don't realize what poorer children face. Maybe someday you will understand."

The little bell rang that ended class. All the children started to rise to leave. We herded them up to say "thank you" to Rabbi Gamaliel. The older children wanted to go swimming once more. Simon and Peter had not been able to beat Mary all week!

I was surprised to see tears in the eyes of some of the children. Little Mary, as you might expect, but even James and John, who had been trouble all week, hated to leave.

Mary turned to me to say good-bye. I only knew her for a week, but I was going to miss her, and the children. We hugged. Then she said, "Maybe someday, we can get this bunch together again."

That's my report. Thanks for listening.

Comment: I spoke earlier of having someone in mind as I wrote a part. For the second sermon of a series on the Trinity, I decided to interview John the Baptist. In the congregation was a young man who weighed about 240 pounds, most of it muscle. He had a very large, full, nearly black beard. Although he is a gentleman in every respect, he is able to hold his own in a car repair shop and on an athletic field. He also happened to be in the church's drama group. I called him early in the week to see if he was going to be at worship. When he said yes, I invited him to do a "dialogue" sermon I was scripting. I told him what it was. He said, "Of course I'll help." I asked if he wanted to see the text before Sunday, and he said, "No." That was okay with me and I think it went well without practice.

As I wrote, I could hear Marshall's voice, its inflections, his vocabulary. It was fun to prepare, and it seemed to be something he could do as easily as we presumed he could.

Rather than doing a straight casting, as I did in the other dramatized story sermons, I transitioned Marshall as Marshall to John the Baptist and back out again at the end.

For those of you who have relatives who are very unimpressed by your religiosity, this kind of sermon, with an intimidating presence like Marshall, can keep them from cracking you up in the middle of your sermon. Mine were at church that morning and they didn't get to me until during the last hymn!

The first sermon in this series on the Trinity is set after Jesus has begun his ministry (see the sermon after next) and the third sermon is based on the second chapter of the Book of Acts and will be found in volume 3.

God, The Son

Matthew 3

Jerry: Marshall, thank you for being willing to help me this morning.

Marshall: That's okay. I would have been here anyway.

Jerry: I asked you to look up John the Baptist so you could have some background for this "sermon." Maybe you can introduce him to us by describing him.

Marshall: Okay. No one really knows what he looked like, except he didn't dress up in good clothes. He wore a cloak made of camel hair and a wide leather belt. I think he had to be a big, burly man, probably with long hair and a beard. A little guy could not have handled the baptizing he did. He had to be strong enough to withstand the current of the river and to hold onto the people in the water with him when he baptized them.

Jerry: How did he do that? Baptize them?

Marshall: Again, no one knows for sure. The word "baptize" literally means to put something completely under water. But it also means putting water on someone.

Jerry: Did John actually "dunk" people?

Marshall: Maybe he did. But the chances are that he had them stand in the water with him and then scooped water with his hand or with a cup and poured it over the person's head.

Jerry: Did John baptize babies?

Marshall: We don't know that for sure either. The Bible doesn't say one way or the other.

Jerry: Based on what you know, if you had been John, would you have baptized babies?

Marshall: I would have baptized anyone! I would have been happy to have the whole people of Israel baptized! What better way to prepare for the coming of the Messiah, the Son of God? A whole nation shaping up, and waiting to let God be their king!

Jerry: Uh, Marshall, that's fairly vague.

Marshall: No, it's not. A typical sermon would be like this: Hey, you dummies, what do you want? To stay out of hell? Is that why you came? What are you scared of? You believe in God, right? You show that off once in a while. I've seen you doing your religious bit, but you're still scared. You can't live with your doubts. You can't live with your bad acts. You don't stop long enough to think what good you are supposed to be doing. Quit running scared. Do all the good you can. Cut out the bad stuff. Keep on messing around and you'll fall apart. The whole country will break up!

Jerry: That's pretty good. But it is still fairly general.

Marshall: Look, you don't always confess everyone's sins for them. Let them plug in their own. Police know when they have been too brutal. Businessmen know when they are cheating someone. People know when they have been uncaring toward their neighbors. Give a more general sermon like John the Baptist did and people will come to you and check off with you about how to handle their lives better.

Jerry: What's baptism for then? You've got them asking the right questions.

Marshall: Yes, but you need to nail down their commitment. Otherwise they'll forget what you got them all riled about.

Jerry: Hey, Marshall, you're getting into this, aren't you?

Marshall: You got that right.

Jerry: Let's proceed like you were John the Baptist and see how that goes. Here you are, baptizing people who are fed up with the way they've let their lives get messed up. Along comes Jesus. How did you handle that?

Marshall: Everyone who came for baptism would have a little conference where they could talk over their concerns before we'd go into the water. When Jesus came, that's what he did.

Jerry: You knew Jesus?

Marshall: He was my cousin. I knew him when he was a little squirt.

Jerry: Did you go to school together?

Marshall: No. I lived in the hill country near Jerusalem and Jesus was from down in Nazareth. We had seen each other during the holidays when Mary and Joseph brought the family up. So when he came to be baptized, I knew he was way ahead of me on matters of religion. So I asked him to baptize me! He said, "No. It is better for the baptizer to baptize than be baptized. You do your thing." So I did.

Jerry: Then what happened?

Marshall: I can only tell you what I saw and heard. You may not believe this. A bird flew down, just as Jesus was walking out onto the shore, and it landed on his shoulder. Jesus and I heard a voice that seemed to be all around us that said, "This is my beloved Son."

Jerry: That is hard to believe.

Marshall: Told you. In our religious training, the bird, the white dove, was a sign of the purity of spirit all people are supposed to have. The doves are the kind that are sacrificed at the Temple. And we were told that if we ever heard a voice saying something good, we were to believe it was God's voice.

Jerry: God's Son? That's what the voice said?

Marshall: Those of us who knew Jesus had no problem with that. That man had integrity that was incredible, and he had compassion that didn't stop. He was scripture-smart, but better than that, he lived it. He was God on the hoof, just like God wants all His children to be.

Jerry: Now wait a minute. If Jesus was God's Son, how can we be God's children?

Marshall: It's a way to describe what is going on. Words don't always do that very well. Let me try this: In the Scriptures, the phrase "sons of God" was used to describe everything from angels to simply being Jews. It also meant someone who worshiped God. Now to worship God is to take Him seriously, to try to do what He hopes for. So all of us who follow God are God's children.

Jerry: But Paul and other New Testament writers use the phrase "Sons of God" in all kinds of ways. Some of my friends in other churches say only "born-again" Christians are children of God. Others refuse to use that phrase about themselves because God has only one son, Jesus.

Marshall: Words! Words! Words! Like I said, words don't always do the job. Everyone is trying to emphasize something important to them, for whatever reason. Me, too.

Jerry: How do you know which way to speak is best?

Marshall: Experience. I grew up as a Nazarite.

Jerry: I thought you said you were from near Jerusalem.

Marshall: A Nazarite is not someone from Nazareth. A Nazarite is someone set aside by his or her parents for God. My hair was not to be cut. I was not to eat grapes or drink wine, and I was devoted to a simple lifestyle dedicated to God. You may have heard of Samson, the strongest man in the Scriptures. He was a Nazarite. So was Samuel, the prophet who anointed Saul and David to be kings of Israel. We were taught we were God's special children.

When I grew up, I spent time with the Essenes at Qumran. They taught that they were the Sons of Light, the Sons of God at war with the Sons of Darkness. Depending on who I talked with, I was either a Son of God because I was learning from the Essenes, or I was a Son of Darkness because I had not formally joined them.

Then I ran into a rabbi who laughed at all this "Son of This/Son of That" talk. He said God was the everlasting Ruler of Israel and didn't need a son to succeed Him!

I was confused, to say the least.

I finally decided how I was going to use the phrase, "Son of God." I decided that any who were led by the Spirit of God, who try to follow the teaching of God, are Sons and Daughters of God. You may not buy that, but it is what I mean by it.

Jerry: But what about Jesus as the Son of God?

Marshall: That's a special thing. I know it's confusing, but I like it.

Jerry: It has something to do with being Messiah, right?

Marshall: You would bring that up. You really want confusion! At Qumran, we learned that there were to be two Messiahs, one descended from Aaron, the priest-brother of Moses, and the other one descended from David the king. The Essenes knew the popular hope for a king Messiah. Everyone wanted a powerful nation once again. But the Essenes knew the story of David and of how he abused his power as king, so they hunted up scripture references to a priestly Messiah. That way, there would be someone to keep an eye on the kingly Messiah.

Jerry: Which was Jesus?

Marshall: He was neither and he was both. He knew all about the texts, and like a number of other rabbis and rebels, was very aware of how many of them applied to himself.

Jerry: Now wait a minute. You mean there were a lot of people who thought they were the Messiah?

Marshall: You bet! It was a tough time. The Roman occupation, the Zealot movement, the dreams of nationhood. Everyone was thinking God had to intervene and bring in His Kingdom. And there were people who tried to take advantage of the times. Oh, yes, there were a lot of them.

Jerry: But you weren't one of them, right?

Marshall: Believe me, when those folks came to hear me preach, I got to thinking maybe I was the Messiah, the special Son of God. But I knew Jesus was around and there was no way I could let myself get the big head.

Jerry: So far as you were concerned, then, Jesus was the Messiah, the Son of the Living God.

Marshall: Not at first. You see, all I knew was that he was sharper, more knowledgeable, and had a way with people that I didn't have. People who heard him preach would tell me their opinions.

Jerry: Which were?

Marshall: He wasn't as angry. He wasn't as negative. We both preached the coming kingdom and the need to repent, but he didn't scare people with their own fear. By the time I learned that lesson, I was in prison.

Jerry: You sent some of your students to check him out, didn't you?

Marshall: They told me he made no claims. He asked them to report to me what they saw.

Jerry: Which was?

Marshall: The lame healed, the lepers cleansed, the unrighteous changing their ways, the discouraged becoming encouraged again, all the things I had been working for. There's nothing like doing what you say you will! He did it.

Jerry: But you were effective. And some of the other Messiah-types must have done well, too. The need certainly sounds like it was there. So how come you picked Jesus out as the "Son of God" and didn't say the same for the others or for yourself?

Marshall: He was my cousin! What reflected well on him reflected well on me!

Jerry: You're serious. Now wait a minute!

Marshall: Had you going there, didn't I?

Jerry: Okay, okay. But I still ask my question. What makes Jesus the Son of God out of all the guys you knew in those days?

Marshall: I kept using him in my conscience to measure how I was doing. Over the years, I found his teachings, his actions, and his attitudes to be right on target. Once in a while, I'd get discouraged and be ready to quit. But I always remembered his respect for my efforts, despite my problems, my mistakes, and my weaknesses. I always felt that God was like that. And here was Jesus doing it.

Jerry *(to congregation)***:** As John the Baptist experienced Jesus, he saw Jesus as the primary example of God's love. Therefore Jesus was the Son of God, as far as he was concerned. But he was literally a relative, as well as a comrade in ministry in the first century. Marshall, I'm going to bring you back and let you reflect, as John the Baptist might if he were alive today.

Marshall: You still have to decide for yourself. I think God acted in history when He worked His divine love in Jesus. There are a lot of ways to describe that action, but I won't go into that right now. But unless you make up your own mind, and then live as though Jesus was your older and wiser brother, I think you're missing something very profound in your life.

Jerry: You sound like a preacher! Say that a little differently.

Marshall: Try this then. God made us all to shine, to bring light and blessing to the world. Jesus blessed us all the way to the cross and even on the cross. He forgave and blessed those around him. That's all I need. What more do you want? All of you, get on out there and bless and forgive. The Son of God is saying, "Go and do likewise."

Jerry: Thank you, Marshall.

25

Comment: Somewhere in my reading, I came across the notion that "executive diseases" like ulcers and headaches were common in Jesus' time among the bureaucrats. With a lead like that, a dimension was added to a story sermon.

Again, the pastor and a lay person speaking from the other side of the sanctuary (at a lectern, perhaps) could conduct the following verbal "correspondence." Or, maybe the pastor could stay out of this completely and turn it over to the laity.

MATTHEW
MATTHEW 9:9-13

Jerusalem, March 18, 13th year of Caesar Tiberius
Office of the Regional Tax Administrator, Antonius Marcellus

To: Chief Tax Collector of the Tiberius region,
Malchus bar Joachim

Dear Mal,
    It is a wonder that old Thaddeus lived long enough to retire.
The Zealots pick off about one tax collector a year around here.
Enclosed herewith is a gold timepiece for him. Give him my best
at the retirement party.
    Pontius Pilate is going bananas up here. The Jews keep baiting
him. He didn't want to come in the first place, but Tiberius is in
Capri, so Sejanus made the assignment. Be glad you are down north,
away from all this political hassle.
    By the way, have you got someone to take old Thaddeus' place?
Let me know. I need it for the records.

Tony

Tiberius, April 1, 13th year of Tiberius Caesar
Office of the Chief Tax Collector, Malchus bar Joachim

To: the Office of the Regional Tax Administrator,
Antonius Marcellus

Dear Tony,
    Keep me out of all that political talk. I don't need the worry!
When Thaddeus retired two weeks ago, no one came in to buy his
territory. The Zealots down here are threatening people. The rabbis

are calling us traitors. None of the men in the village are even willing to take turns watching the office over there at Capernaum. It is very intimidating right now. I'll let you know as soon as I can get someone to go in there.

What's good for an upset stomach?

Mal

Jerusalem, April 15, 13th year of Caesar Tiberius
Office of the Regional Tax Administrator, Antonius Marcellus

To: Chief Tax Collector of the Tiberius region,
Malchus bar Joachim

Dear Mal,

Better find someone quick. Pilate is already on my back about the decline in taxes from your area.

Have you tried rice and tea for that stomach of yours?

Tony

Tiberius, May 3, 13th year of Tiberius Caesar
Office of the Chief Tax Collector, Malchus bar Joachim

To: the Office of the Regional Tax Administrator,
Antonius Marcellus

Dear Tony,

I tried the rice and tea all winter. Didn't help much. Got the runs. You got all the high-powered medical people up there. Please check with them.

Finally got someone to fill in. His name is Levi, but he calls himself Matthew. Usually when a guy starts collecting taxes, he changes his name to a Roman or Greek name. But he took another Jewish name. The locals up there never saw him before. He came over from Cana. The locals thought he was a repair man. He had carpentry tools along and remodeled the office. He got acquainted with them, went out to eat with them, and told pretty good stories. They got to liking him. They lost their sandals when they found out he was the new tax collector. At first they were resentful, but he has such a fair way about him, they began cooperating. He's been taking in the back taxes so we should be caught up now.

Mal

Jerusalem, May 30, 13th year of Caesar Tiberius
Office of the Regional Tax Administrator, Antonius Marcellus

To: Chief Tax Collector of the Tiberius region,
Malchus bar Joachim

Dear Mal,

Amazing! You're all caught up! That Matthew must be something else. I should have a winner like him up here.

For that stomach and your other problem, how about trying some goat's milk and cheese.

By the way, that spook Caligula came through here. I don't believe that man. Sneaking around at night and looking in windows, at the army barracks yet! He's nuts! But he's Tiberius' nephew. Unless Tiberius has a boy of his own, Caligula gets to be emperor. Tiberius is already 69 so we may be stuck with a crazy.

I've been having a lot of headaches lately. I find it hard to work when I get one. Tell me what you do for them down there.

Tony

Tiberius, July 1, 13th year of Tiberius Caesar
Office of the Chief Tax Collector, Malchus bar Joachim

To: the Office of the Regional Tax Administrator,
Antonius Marcellus

Dear Tony,

Matthew's a clever guy, but you think you got headaches! He's writing poetry. He was up in the hills all last week instead of watching the Damascus-Acre road office. He even sent me a copy of his poems about being tempted by the Devil. I had to switch him with the guy who handles the taxes of the fishermen. I think he got the hint.

The cheese helped and the stomach is not as fiery as it has been. But I still don't sleep too much.

Caligula came through here two weeks ago. The next day, one of King Herod's advisors went on trial for treason. The word is that the guy was set up by Caligula, but there's no proof. The advisor was crucified yesterday. Everyone is keeping a low profile right now. Herod doesn't need help to be paranoid.

For your headaches, all I can say is take a nap every day. The roots and leaves around here don't work, so most of the headache sufferers around here just try to sleep them off.

Mal

Jerusalem, July 30, 13th year of Caesar Tiberius
Office of the Regional Tax Administrator, Antonius Marcellus

To: Chief Tax Collector of the Tiberius region,
Malchus bar Joachim

Dear Mal,
The naps work, when I can get to sleep. Sometimes the headaches go away. But sometimes they keep me awake and I don't handle it very well. The secretaries keep their distance when I have a bad headache.

Your figures aren't too good this last report. Is that Matthew again, or what?

Tony

Tiberius, August 15, 13th year of Tiberius Caesar
Office of the Chief Tax Collector, Malchus bar Joachim

To: the Office of the Regional Tax Administrator,
Antonius Marcellus

Dear Tony,

Matthew's doing okay. I guess he likes the outdoor work much better. Maybe it's easier for him to do his writing while the fishermen are out to sea. The merchants go to the office out on the highway any time of the day or night. That toll booth work is pretty tough, I'll admit. The guy in there now complained the other day. He wants a break. Maybe I can get him and Matthew to rotate or something.

The reason for the drop in taxes is that Herod's troops are stopping some of the traffic on the highway, looking for Zealots who are trying to slip out of the country. Herod's making things hot and the leaders are trying to cross the border. So that slows everything down.

Some of the merchants threatened to burn our tax office on the highway if Herod doesn't ease up. Our guy hasn't heard that news yet. I hope he doesn't.

Can you get Pilate to lean on Herod so we can straighten out this mess?

Stomach's gone crazy. Even goat's milk doesn't help any more.

Mal

Jerusalem, September 18, 14th year of Caesar Tiberius
Office of the Regional Tax Administrator, Antonius Marcellus

To: Chief Tax Collector of the Tiberius region,
Malchus bar Joachim

Dear Mal,

Sorry about the delay. With the holiday yesterday, and no one wanting to work until it was over, I finally got to Pilate this morning. He doesn't like Herod, but he's also not anxious to get into a problem with him, either. He sent an emissary down there this afternoon. He said he would have to reassign Herod's soldiers to Caesarea by the sea if the taxes from your area didn't pick up. He hopes that will work.

These headaches are killing me. No one up here has anything that works either. I've tried to knock myself out with wine and that does help for a few hours. But then I wake up with an awful hangover on top of the headache. Somewhere, there's got to be relief.

Tony

Tiberius, December 20, 14th year of Tiberius Caesar
Office of the Chief Tax Collector, Malchus bar Joachim

To: the Office of the Regional Tax Administrator,
Antonius Marcellus

Dear Tony,

Sorry to be so slow in writing back. Pilate's emissary didn't help matters. Why doesn't Pilate realize the Jews hate his guts and don't trust him? He sent this jerk of a Roman "gentleman" who doesn't believe anyone else in the world is a human being. Herod ran him off, as you know, and Pilate sent him back with some Roman legionnaires. Herod didn't even have to send his troops out. Farmers, fishermen, even the merchants, set up a roadblock. The snob solved the whole problem. He ran! The soldiers didn't like him either so they just turned around. End of confrontation.

By then, Herod had picked up the ringleader of the Zealots, a guy named Barabbas, so he let the highway reopen without any more searches.

I got Matthew to switch and take the toll booth for a series of two-month turns. That seems to be working out.

My wife tells me that the only time she gets headaches is from drinking red wine. Check that out. My stomach is better now. But it sure hurt when those soldiers came down from Jerusalem.

Mal

Jerusalem, June 18, 14th year of Caesar Tiberius
Office of the Regional Tax Administrator, Antonius Marcellus

To: Chief Tax Collector of the Tiberius region,
Malchus bar Joachim

Dear Mal,

My headaches have subsided, too. It's nice to have some peace and quiet for once.

There was one of those treason trials here a couple months ago. But it was an army officer so the tax department wasn't threatened.

I tried cutting out the wine, and I have had fewer side-of-the-head headaches. But the front-of-the-head headaches increased for a while until I found some pure water to drink.

I notice your taxes have dropped off again. What's that about?

Tony

Tiberius, July 20, 14th year of Tiberius Caesar
Office of the Chief Tax Collector, Malchus bar Joachim

To: the Office of the Regional Tax Administrator,
Antonius Marcellus

Dear Tony,

Those Zealots again. They have been riling up the people. They say Caesar shouldn't have such a big army and so many weapons. They're tired of paying taxes for such a big defense budget.

They are also upset that the aqueduct system has been disrupted. They aren't getting the water we promised them and that their taxes paid for. And they've gotten back no money from Jerusalem or Rome for repairing bridges and roads. They are tired of paying out and getting none of the normal results of working through government. Can you see if Pilate will do something about it?

I heard a crazy story from Matthew the other day. He said a third cousin of his came to his wedding two years ago and turned water into wine. And here we want wine turned into water, you for your headache, and me for my stomach! Isn't that crazy?

Mal

34

Jerusalem, September 18, 15th year of Caesar Tiberius
Office of the Regional Tax Administrator, Antonius Marcellus

To: Chief Tax Collector of the Tiberius region,
Malchus bar Joachim

Dear Mal,

Happy New Year! Well, Tiberius is now 71 and he made his fifteenth anniversary as Caesar. I don't know how he's made it so far.

It has gotten crazy around here again. Everyone but Pilate is involved with another woman, except for me, of course. You and your stomach, me and my head, the bureaucrats and their women, you don't suppose problems go with our kind of job, do you?

Tony

Tiberius, October 15, 15th year of Tiberius Caesar
Office of the Chief Tax Collector, Malchus bar Joachim

To: the Office of the Regional Tax Administrator,
Antonius Marcellus

Dear Tony,

It is almost as crazy down here. One of the caravans coming through last month had a shipment of a drug called opium. The merchant was low on cash, he said, so he gave some to the tax collector and told him how to use it. He'd been having headaches, too, so he tried it, rather than send it as payment in kind.

His headaches went away, but so did his attention span. When he was on the opium, he didn't collect taxes. When he was off, he was showing the others around our area how it worked.

The only guy who didn't get caught up in it was Matthew. He said he didn't need anything like that to relieve him. He said his imagination did so much for him that he didn't need artificial means to get to sleep, get rid of pain, or get a vision.

He told me he saw his third cousin recently and heard that if you have the faith of a grain of mustard seed, you could move mountains.

He said he had an image explode in his mind of the tiny seed developing into a tree-sized shrub and which had a root system just as large under the soil. He said we all had to grow where people can't see it as much as we do where people can see it. He said the growth comes with study of our law, our poetry, our prophets, and our traditions and history. He said growth comes with meeting regularly with others who seek to grow. He said that's how roots develop.

So he has the guys over for dinner once a week. Several have stopped the opium and some have quit seeing their women. I think Matthew has something good going. My stomach has felt better since I started attending. Maybe we'll come out of this opium craziness yet.

Mal

Jerusalem, November 10, 15th year of Caesar Tiberius
Office of the Regional Tax Administrator, Antonius Marcellus

To: Chief Tax Collector of the Tiberius region,
Malchus bar Joachim

Dear Mal,
That opium merchant didn't have money here, either. Gave out the opium and all the headaches and womanizing here stopped soon after. But so did the work. Pilate is furious. He thinks Herod is behind this. Even though he is a ruler in your areas, he is still a Jew, and Pilate thinks Herod has plotted to undermine the Romans here with the opium.

I don't understand that root/seeds thing your friend, Matthew, told you about. How can imagination work for a headache?

Tony

Tiberius, December 1, 15th year of Tiberius Caesar
Office of the Chief Tax Collector, Malchus bar Joachim

To: the Office of the Regional Tax Administrator,
Antonius Marcellus

Dear Tony,

Matthew left his office three weeks ago and is now part of a group of followers of his third cousin. He just up and left. I can't blame him. All the hassles, all the grief! I almost pulled out myself that very night.

Jesus, his third cousin, has been teaching in the village up here. Matthew met him a couple months ago when he was collecting taxes from the fishermen. Because of his work schedule, he was able to see Jesus in several of the villages without interfering with his tax collecting. He began keeping notes on what Jesus said. Up until three weeks ago, Matthew kept his distance. He knew the rabbis' attitudes about tax collectors being the scum of the earth. But he was fascinated by Jesus' teachings. He told us all about them at our weekly dinner meetings.

Three weeks ago, Jesus was on the road passing the toll booth. He spotted Matthew, came over, and said, "Come, follow me." And he just left. I didn't know about it until that night. We all met at Matthew's as usual, only this time, he had Jesus with him.

Was that a shocker, a rabbi eating with all the tax collectors in the area! Local lawyers and rabbis heard about it and interrupted our dinner. When they got done calling Jesus and us all kinds of names, Jesus quietly told them, "Those who are well do not need a physician, but those who are sick." He shut them up with that. You could have heard a pin drop. Well, they left.

More next time. Something just came up and I want to get this into the pouch.

Mal

Jerusalem, December 10, 15th year of Caesar Tiberius
Office of the Regional Tax Administrator, Antonius Marcellus

To: Chief Tax Collector of the Tiberius region,
Malchus bar Joachim

Dear Mal,
  What's happening? Your collections are still good. But I haven't
heard from you.

Tony

Tiberius, December 25, 15th year of Tiberius Caesar
Office of the Chief Tax Collector, Malchus bar Joachim

To: the Office of the Regional Tax Administrator,
Antonius Marcellus

Dear Tony,
  Herod's soldiers came through here like a herd of camels. I
thought they were going to close us down and arrest us. But they
were looking for Jesus. Jesus and Matthew and the others left soon
after that dinner we had at Capernaum so Herod missed them completely. Any more episodes like that and my stomach would have
turned into a furnace!
  Except this time, I wasn't really scared and my stomach didn't
hurt.   .
  Jesus was so reassuring about us as God's family, as worthwhile, as valuable, that I did not even think to panic when the soldiers came.
  If I had been smart like Matthew, I'd have gone with Jesus
when they left. But Jesus made us realize not everyone is a rabbi, a
teacher, or writer like Matthew. There are times he needs certain
skills and certain personalities to follow him by leaving everything
behind. But there are ministries to perform where we are, and in
what others of us are already doing. Obey God and the Kingdom
of God happens!
  Sorry about this preaching, but Jesus really fired us up, and
my stomach's a lot better. Keep your eyes open for Jesus when he
comes to Jerusalem. Maybe he can help you, too.

Mal

Comment: It was the beginning of summer and I was chomping at the bit to do some more story sermons. Only I was interested in doing something that explained the Trinity, something that might prove more memorable than other sermons I had tried on the subject. For Father's Day, I tackled the First Person of the Trinity.

God, The Father
Matthew 6:1-8

"Jake! Jacob ben Jacob! Is that you?"

Samuel's voice was very excited. The peculiar puffy eyelids could only be those of his childhood friend. The man turned and looked at him.

"Sammy? Sammy, my old friend!"

They gave each other a huge hug and a big kiss. Samuel had not expected such a great blessing.

No one else in the milling crowd paid much attention to them as they greeted each other so warmly.

"I don't believe it, I don't believe it," Samuel repeated. "How good to see you!"

"And you, too," Jacob replied. And then the two separated, facing each other. Their manners returned. "Grace and peace to you from Almighty God," Samuel said. "Peace be with you, too," Jacob responded.

"That's not how to reply, Jake. Don't you remember in synagogue ..." Samuel started.

Jacob waved him off. "You haven't changed a bit! You were a rabbi even before bar mitzvah!"

The two men laughed, and looked for a shady spot to sit down.

"What are you doing here in Nazareth?" Jacob asked his rabbi friend.

"The head rabbi in Jerusalem thought it would be good if I came down north to think over my spiritual roots. He ordered me to take a pilgrimage to Mount Tabor. I guess he had enough of my questions about his administration. I don't like how impersonal our leaders are getting. I don't understand it. But the Lord will decide among us who is right and who is wrong. Enough of my troubles. What are you doing here? The last time I saw you was just after bar mitzvah in Bethlehem. That's thirty years ago! What are you doing? How's your mother? Are you married?"

"Whoa! Slow down, my old friend!" Jacob responded. "It's a long story. Where do I begin? We left Bethlehem so my father could find work. After the census was over, it seemed like everything dried up so father wanted to try Jerusalem. But not long after we moved there, he died."

"Too much wine?" Samuel asked.

"Too much wine," Jacob whispered. "His death came none too soon. He had been mean to Mom and to me for years, and he was terrible when he had been drinking. After we moved, he got worse, drinking all the time, and vicious all the time. I got away from it because I apprenticed with a carpenter. Mom walked the streets to stay out of his way. She stayed at our carpenter's shop, finding excuses to be there. One day she fainted. When my boss' wife opened her cloak to help her breathe, she found terrible bruises on her and took her into the house-part of the building. My father was in a drunken rage and came looking for her at our shop. When he didn't find her, he came after me. My boss yelled, 'Grab his left arm and pull.' He was trying to grab the right arm. 'Now walk him backward,' he yelled. With me on one side and my boss on the other, each holding out one of his arms and walking him backward around the shop and finally out onto the street, my father calmed down. We took him to the rabbi's house, but the rabbi said he had a right to go after his wife for running away. I couldn't believe it. I haven't been to synagogue since, all respect to you, my friend. Anyway, when we left the rabbi's, my father collapsed on the street. We took him back to the shop, but he died before we could get any help for him."

"God could no longer tolerate his sin," Samuel began.

"God took his time about it," Jacob said bitterly.

"So, how is your mother?"

"She's okay. She has been a widow and not remarried. I don't believe she trusts her judgment about men. But outside of that, she has lived with me and my wife and family."

"Two women in your household? That must make things pretty tense."

41

"No, fortunately, Mom's been very careful about that. She and Muriel got along very well. She lets Muriel be in charge and Muriel asks her advice on nearly everything."

"So what are you doing in Nazareth?" Samuel wondered.

"My second cousin Joseph and his family stayed with us in Jerusalem after a trip they made to Egypt. He wanted a helper in his carpenter shop here in Nazareth so Mom and I came north with them. That's my story. Tell me yours," Jacob concluded.

"Well, my dad is dead, too, but not of wine."

"No, I wouldn't have thought that. Of apoplexy, maybe, but not wine," Jacob inserted.

"That's close. You remember how strict my father was. Even though he wasn't a rabbi, he wore these phylacteries and made us wear them all the time. When we asked him why none of the other kids wore them, he said they were disobedient to God and that they would suffer the consequences. We asked him what the consequences were. And he talked about them being thrown into the Valley of Hinnom outside Jerusalem, the garbage dump where fires smoldered every night and where the lepers lived."

"Did you think I would end up there?" Jacob asked.

"You were my friend, but, yes, I was really sure God would dump you there. I was so scared about it that I couldn't even tell you."

"What about now?" Jacob asked.

"Believe it or not, I don't know. This is what the head rabbi has against me. I was beginning to doubt that the Lord God would deal with everyone so strictly." Samuel reached up, lifted the little box strapped to his forehead, wiped the sweat from his brow, and then went on. "The head rabbi said that such doubt had no place in the life of a rabbi. He said God was the Lord, the giver of the Law, the enforcer when there were violations of the Law. God was not to be doubted. We rabbis were not to doubt, lest we lead others to doubt. But I do doubt. I saw my dad struggle with his beliefs and how they did not quite fit with his life experiences."

"Like what, Sammy?" Jacob asked.

"Like the time my mother accidentally spilled milk on our meat. We didn't have much, so Mom washed it off and cooked the meat for supper. My father nearly had a fit. He was convinced the meat was unclean because of the contact with the milk and he wouldn't let us eat it. There was no reasoning with him. At the time, I agreed with my father, but my mother went ahead and ate it anyway."

"Sounds like your parents."

"But my father was so angry, he yelled, 'I divorce you. I divorce you. I divorce you.' Mom left the room. A few minutes later, she left the house. And we never saw her again. To this day, I don't know what happened to her. My father stood there for the longest time. 'I'm right,' he said. 'I'm right. I'm right. I'm right.' he said. After that he never spoke another word about it. And I never did either ... 'til now. Right after I began studies for the rabbinate, my father took very sick. On his deathbed, his last words were, 'I'm right.' You know, until just now, I thought he was. But now, I don't know if I believe that either."

Samuel sat quietly for a long time. Jacob let him be.

Samuel broke his own silence. "What's the crowd about?"

"Oh, these people came out to hear Jesus."

"Who's that?"

"He's a young rabbi, my cousin's son."

"All I need now is to hear another rabbi," Samuel said.

"Don't worry. He doesn't talk too long, and he tells good stories."

"This many people came to hear him?"

"Not all the time. But he also does healing and a lot of these people are here for that. They couldn't care less about what he says. Oh, there he is. Stay, please."

Reluctantly, Samuel stayed. Jesus spoke about ten minutes. Then the people swarmed all over him, seeking his healing touch. It got to be too much, so Jesus, looking very weary, climbed down from the little mound where he had stood to preach, and headed for the nearby mountain.

People were angry with Jesus and swore at him, but finally, they began leaving.

Samuel followed the departing Jesus with his eyes.

Jacob said, "I know where he's headed. Do you want to go?"

"Yes, I do. Will he talk with me?"

"We can try."

The two men moved through the diminishing crowd and went after him.

Up on the mountain, Jesus was talking to his disciples when Samuel and Jacob found them.

"Do not be like them, for your Father knows what you need before you ask him," Jesus was saying.

Jesus stopped as he saw them approach. "Grace and peace to you from almighty God," Samuel said. "Grace and peace to you from God our heavenly Father," Jesus replied.

Samuel winced when Jesus said the word, "Father."

"Rabbi, pardon my intrusion, but how did you come to your beliefs?" Samuel rightfully challenged, as one rabbi to another.

Jesus looked at this troubled middle-aged rabbi. Tired though he himself was, he offered him a hand, inviting him to join the circle, and made a response. "My colleague, let me ask you a question. How did you come by yours?"

"By learning from the teachers at the school for rabbis."

"That is a good place to learn about our faith. While I could not get to the school, I learned from rabbis around here."

"Which of them taught you about prayer? Surely the Lord God wants us to pray. But if He already knows our needs before we ask, as I heard you teaching a few moments ago, then we don't need to pray at all."

"You have spoken correctly," Jesus said, surprising everyone. "What is your understanding?"

"Well, God is our Lord. We must approach Him with awe, reverence, respect ..."

"And," Jesus interjected, "fear."

"Yes," Samuel replied, "fear. We cannot really approach God. He is perfect. We are not. He cannot tolerate sin or wrong. He can only receive those who are righteous." Suddenly Samuel felt very odd. He knew his words were right, but his heart felt strange.

"You have heard it said by men of old, 'Love God and hate your enemies ...' " Jesus began.

"Jesus, I don't hate God. I hate ... I hate ..."

44

Samuel fell into heavy sobbing. Jesus and Jacob knelt next to him and put their arms around him.

"I hate my father," Samuel began when he caught his breath. "And Jacob's father. How could men be so cruel, one with violence, one with righteousness! If you had said God was 'Mother,' I would have ... I would have ..."

"Been upset," Jesus remarked. "Listen, my friend. God is love, not just righteousness. God is patience, not violence. How do the psalms read?"

"He will not keep His wrath forever. Like a father pities his children ..." Samuel repeated.

"You got it. I knew of Jacob's father," Jesus said, "and I can understand why he has not always heard what I said. I think you must have had a father who was too rigid. My father was a good man. That's why I address God as Father. God is good and I find it natural to talk of God and to God as though he were my dad."

"I don't know, Rabbi," Samuel said to Jesus. "Help me in my unbelief."

Comment: One of the real treats I've had as a minister is to have my daughter help me with one of my story sermons. In her spiritual pilgrimage, she had found herself in a group of youth led by a charismatic. The youth were good friends, and the charismatic was a nice person, as far as I knew, though he was not affiliated with any local church.

In preparing the text, I found myself using that bit of history. I asked her to read it over and see if it was okay. She agreed to do this little drama. She read it over again in the car on the way to the church. There were a couple of spots where I was worried about the timing. But she felt at home with the text, which had come easily because I could hear her saying those things as I wrote.

Typically, when I preach in a small, flat-floored church, I sit on a kitchen stool (no, it is not a bar stool!). When I do stories, especially with a tight script, I have the text on a music stand, set low enough so I can have as much eye contact with the congregation as I can. My daughter decided it would be smoother if we both read it from the one text. It worked nicely for us in that setting.

I introduced myself as the 49-year-old Gamaliel, now a widely respected rabbi in Jerusalem. And my daughter played the nameless sixteen-year-old daughter of the rabbi. The approximate date of the conversation is 34 A.D., just before Paul's conversion experience on the road to Damascus, but several years after Pentecost and the development of the church in Jerusalem.

THE MAN BORN BLIND
JOHN 9

Daughter: Dad, have you got a minute?

Rabbi: Of course, come on in.

Daughter: We need to talk.

Rabbi: Saul's gone, right?

Daughter: Dad, quit trying to read my mind.

Rabbi: What else would a lovely sixteen-year-old like you talk about?

Daughter: Oh, Dad!

Rabbi: I'm sorry. I didn't mean that. Start where you want.

Daughter: Well, Dad, I'm sorry Saul is gone. And I'm glad he's gone. I mean ... That's not what I came to talk about. I'm ... I'm thinking about becoming a follower of the Way.

Rabbi: *(Silence)*

Daughter: Well ... say something. Do you hate me? What?

Rabbi: No, I don't hate you at all, Honey. I'm just not sure what to say.

Daughter: I can come back later.

Rabbi: No, stay. I'm just sorting out a few things. What got you started?

Daughter: It was six years ago.

Rabbi: Six years!?

Daughter: I was downtown shopping when I saw a strange thing happen. A rabbi stopped to give first aid to a blind man. I had seen him many times before.

Rabbi: The rabbi?

Daughter: No, the blind man. Everyone knew he was that way from birth, so no one tried to help him medically. In fact, no one tried to help him at all.

Rabbi: Who was the rabbi?

Daughter: Jesus.

Rabbi: Oh, yes. I remember that story. That's the one where Jesus made the point that it wasn't the parents' fault that their son was blind. He said it was an opportunity for him to demonstrate the power of God. I remember that story well. It was the turning point in my relationship with Saul.

Daughter: I thought you two got along very well.

Rabbi: I think we should always try to get along with everyone. But that can be extremely difficult. That incident drove a wedge between Saul and me that we never overcame. I'm surprised he stayed on as a student with me as long as he did. But go on with your story.

Daughter: No, I'll do mine after you tell me about Saul.

Rabbi: Well ... okay.

Daughter: How did the blind man incident cause you a problem? You were in Joppa at the time.

Rabbi: My, you remember my comings and goings better than I do. It came up as a class project. Saul had heard about it and we discussed it thoroughly.

Daughter: I told him about it.

Rabbi: I wondered ... because he hadn't seen it himself. We had to deal with it hypothetically. I wish I'd known you told him. I would have had you come to class.

Daughter: But girls aren't allowed ...

Rabbi: That's just a tradition. I guess I didn't realize how interested you were ...

Daughter: I didn't ... You were so ... No, I won't put you on a guilt trip.

Rabbi: I appreciate that ... As Saul told the story, it was obvious he agreed with the way the Pharisees handled the matter. Jesus had done the first aid on the Sabbath. Saul thought that was the kind of work which is against our Sabbath laws. When I said that mercy is not work, he argued that God made the Sabbath rest for good reason, and that the man could have been helped the next day. He was using my argument against workaholics and twisting it so it would prevent helping his neighbor. I hope someday Saul realizes that actions which show love of neighbor are more true to

49

God's law than keeping Pharisaic law. I remember telling him that he who loves his neighbor fulfills the law.

Daughter: Jesus said that, too.

Rabbi: But Saul was adamant. Maybe it was because he comes from a wealthy family and had all that Greek education before coming here. I don't know. He does get rather arrogant and hard-headed sometimes. He argued that a sinner could not heal anyone. And Saul seemed to think no one is as sinless as himself because of his conscientiousness. In fact, Saul didn't really believe the man had been blind from birth. He thought it was a hoax, even though the Pharisees who investigated came back saying the blindness was true. He thought God's judgment should come down on the parents for lying. And he got very angry when he talked of how the formerly blind man challenged the Pharisees for not knowing why and how Jesus could have healed him. Saul thinks the law is a very strict master, assigned by God to be our custodian who knows how to take care of us better than we do ourselves. Anyway, I called him a pinhead for being so narrow-minded.

Daughter: You what?

Rabbi: Called him a pinhead.

Daughter: Really?

Rabbi: No, not really. I know a little Greek so I played with his name and called him Paul instead of Saul. In Greek, "Paul" means "little." He took offense and something in our relationship died. He has resented me ever since. I didn't mean to hurt him. But I was trying to say he was too confined in his attitude about God and the Law. Maybe someday he'll open up a little. He's off to Damascus to investigate the Christians there and ... I think it's time we talked about you.

Daughter: Well, I think I'm one of those Christians Saul is so uptight about. I mean ... the way you mentioned Jesus' name before, I wonder if you ... well ...

Rabbi: I am a good Jew. Jesus was a good Jew. Saul, well ... but you ... you have been a good Jew, so tell me ...

Daughter: Like it goes back to when I saw Jesus help that man. He reached out to him. I wouldn't have done it because of the law which tries to prevent our becoming unclean. And I got used to not doing anything for that blind man or anyone else, for that matter.

Rabbi: That's not entirely true. You help me and you help around the house.

Daughter: For a price. That's how I earn my spending money.

Rabbi: I know. I didn't mean to restrict my view of your helpfulness to stuff we pay you for. You've worked down at the synagogue. You've helped some of the kids at school.

Daughter: Thanks for trying, but I don't help that much. That's why Jesus impressed me that day. We all have the power to help, God's power to help. Jesus showed me that I shouldn't hold back God's power to help just because our religion prohibits it.

Rabbi: I have been gone too much. The Jewish religion is a religion of compassion, of helping, of love.

Daughter: How come you are one of the only ones I ever hear who says that? All I hear is "obey this law, obey that law." That's why I want to join the Christians.

Rabbi: What's the big deal? I taught Jesus everything he knew!

Daughter: Oh, Dad! *(Gamaliel joins his daughter in saying "Oh, Dad.")*

Rabbi: I'm teasing. What I heard him say is very much what I understand Jewish religion to be. I praise God whenever anyone puts the love of God and neighbor above law and tradition, without losing respect for the lessons reflected in the law and traditions.

Daughter: Can you repeat that?

Rabbi: I doubt it! Seriously, every rabbi who teaches looking at all our rules and practices in the light of our love of God and neighbor is on the right track.

Daughter: But our religion is so stuffy. The Christians do exciting things. They have meals together regularly. They study the scriptures all the time. They pray all the time. Like we don't do that at home. No offense ... but I really like being with those people. And I get so much out of it.

Rabbi: That's great. I'm very pleased you have found something for your religious life that pleases you.

Daughter: Dad, I ... I speak in tongues.

51

Rabbi: *(Brief silence followed by)* Oh?

Daughter: That's not crazy, is it? I mean like it's okay. I've done it only a few times and like ... It's okay and everything. I really enjoyed it. Dad?

Rabbi: I'm thinking again. I have never done it, at least not in the way you described it.

Daughter: How do you know about it?

Rabbi: I've been around. I've talked with some of the church elders who have spoken in tongues in their groups. They told me it is primarily a devotional moment, a private prayer between the believer and God. I can go along with that. Who can dictate how we should talk with God personally? Sometimes I can't put words on my pain when I pray. I just sigh. Sometimes I scream when I'm alone with God. And that makes me feel better, too. I just don't let my mouth go. Does that sound wrong?

Daughter: Of course not, Dad. Like you have the right to be yourself with God, just like everybody else. What else did you learn?

Rabbi: The elders commented that some of these who speak in tongues become addicted because it is the only thing that they have going for them. And sometimes they make a big deal out of how much the Spirit gives them. And they can go on an ego trip. New Christians may come in looking for a place to feel important and so they buy into the ego trip. Do you follow me?

Daughter: They can't make it at school or work so they try to become big in the church?

Rabbi: The Church should always have room for strugglers, but the elders say the Spirit gives many gifts, not just tongues, gifts of teaching, music, healing, organizing. And all of these are backed up by God's love.

Daughter: Should I give up speaking in tongues?

Rabbi: No, just because a few abuse the gift doesn't mean it should be given up. So far, I haven't heard anything from you that you have become an abuser.

Daughter: I don't think I am either. Like I don't think anyone else in our group is.

Rabbi: That's probably true.

Daughter: The group tells me that speaking in tongues comes from the Holy Spirit. Is it?

Rabbi: I'm told Jesus was asked if he was from God, and he replied, "Look at what I'm doing. Is that from God?" If speaking in tongues is from God, it does what God wants it to do. And I can't argue against it. For some it gives freedom from the pressure of traditional rigid practices and lets them be themselves. It lets some people express the inexpressible. Others don't always get these results, but for those who do, I see God's hand in it. When God is at work, we are wise not to interfere.

Daughter: Didn't you say something like that last year at the Sanhedrin when they held their hearing on Peter and John?

Rabbi: I'm glad they listened. Or we would have had two murders on our hands. The Pharisees were out for blood. I ... don't know if you should risk getting involved ...

Daughter: What else did the elders say?

Rabbi: They said that while some get their jollies by speaking in tongues in the church meetings, not very many in the group get anything out of it. It's like showing off your ability to speak a foreign language. Without an interpreter, who knows what you said? I've heard the elders say they'd rather say a few words that help the group than say many words in tongues that are meaningless to the group.

Daughter: Like I should quit the tongue thing?

Rabbi: No, just be sure it helps you and it helps others.

Daughter: Like Jesus helped the blind man despite our religious laws.

Rabbi: Like that. You got it.

Daughter: *(Hugs Dad)* Thanks a lot. *(Returns to her seat)*

Rabbi: You bet.

Comment: Sometimes a story is the only way to get across to others what is happening and how it could be handled better. At least, I thought that when I prepared this short story.

A friend was accused of something by someone who refused to bring formal charges. But the church leaders went ahead by bringing the formal charges themselves. As one of several people trying to help the friend, I hoped this telling of a biblical story would provide a bridge for people from both sides to see the event more Christianly without either side having to admit mishandling.

As far as I can tell, it had very little impact. But maybe, outside of the emotionally-loaded context in which it was attempted, it may speak to others now.

Jewish law provided for the protection of the accused from arbitrary or false accusation. Justice required two valid witnesses to any capital crime, of which adultery was one. No one who had a conflict of interest was supposed to be allowed to take part as a judge or presider. With such interesting parallels to U.S. constitutional law, it was not hard to touch on our own sense of injustice in telling of the trial in the story.

ON CASTING THE FIRST STONE
JOHN 7:53–8:11

The village could have been any of those that sat in the hills around Jerusalem. It had its normal people. It had its odd people. It had its leaders. It had its quiet ones. It had its good people. And it had its bad people. And it had people like you and me, with a little mixture of all of that.

Miriam was a widow. She was a very lonely person. In Jewish tradition, an unmarried brother was supposed to continue the marriage of his dead brother's widow. Miriam had not remarried after her husband died because her husband had no brother. She scratched out a living as one of several serving people cooking and housecleaning for one of the leaders. She was a very quiet person. She was hardly noticed as she came and went.

Johanna was Miriam's neighbor. Actually, she fancied herself everyone's neighbor. She was friendly. She was generous. She listened very well. She would say, "Tell me all about it." And the unwary would, only to find out later that the secrets had become common knowledge. Johanna was a gossip. But she was so friendly and so generous of her time and attention that her flaw was given little notice.

Eli was also Miriam's neighbor. He was a widower. He loved to talk. He was very musical. But he was also very mixed up. Eli liked Miriam very much. She never talked back. She never interrupted him when he was talking. She seemed to like his songs. He was over there to see Miriam as often as she would let him.

Eli also would stop to chat with Johanna. Ever the neighbor, Johanna would ask how Miriam was and Eli would say glowing things about the quiet widow, how she was so kind to him, how she would listen to his songs. After a few times of such conversation, Johanna began to press Eli. "Ah, Eli," she'd say, "it must be wonderful to be in love." Eli, not to be seen as inept in matters of the heart, began to add a little to his stories of how he and Miriam passed time. Though Miriam continued to be the quiet gracious widow to Eli's chatting and singing, Eli's description of their relationship took a far deeper turn that would have shocked Miriam if she had known. Johanna would, in turn, tell other folks about the "silent waters that run so deep."

Another neighbor let word slip to Miriam what Johanna was saying about her. Miriam was terribly hurt and went to her friend Johanna and confronted her. Johanna was deeply offended and denied that she would ever say such a thing. Offering Miriam a generous gift of bread, Johanna was able to be reconciled with her. And Miriam never said another word about it.

A few days later, however, both women were at the market. Johanna tried to get Miriam's attention across the way but Miriam was preoccupied and didn't notice her neighbor. Johanna took it as a slight — that Miriam was getting too big for her britches. When Miriam returned home and Johanna saw her, she confronted the quiet widow with her slight. Miriam apologized profusely, saying she hadn't meant to hurt her friend. But Johanna's nose was still out of joint.

The next day, as Eli came by, Johanna asked him how things were going with Miriam. Eli rhapsodized about Miriam, describing vividly acts that went beyond all his previous fantasies.

Johanna went immediately to the Rabbi.

The Rabbi was shocked and immediately called upon Eli to discover the truth. Eli was so enamored of his fantasies that he shared them with the Rabbi. Eli did not go to synagogue, so the Rabbi did not know him very well. He felt that Eli was being led on by this Miriam, about whom he had heard rumors. Eli was seen as the credible one.

Now the Rabbi wanted to show he was modern in the best sense of that word. He wanted to conduct an investigation. So he invited several elders from the synagogue to join him for an interview with Miriam. The Rabbi said to her, when he invited her to the gathering, "Trust us. We want to help. We just want to talk things over." Miriam had no idea why she was invited. She felt she had better go or she might get into trouble.

When she entered the room, she faced ten men and the Rabbi. This was very frightening to her. The Rabbi tried to put her at ease. He asked her about her life as a widow. The men all nodded as she spoke of the loneliness, missing her husband, passes being made by men, bills, and the heavy chores she had to handle.

"Isn't Eli some help to you?" the Rabbi asked.

"Oh, yes," Miriam replied. "He talks with me and he sings his little songs. He helps repair little things at my house. He's such a love."

"We thank you for coming and sharing your story with us. We understand much better what is happening. You may leave now," the Rabbi said. She looked at the faces of the men and was glad to excuse herself. After she left, there was quick agreement. They had her confession.

Then they brought in Eli and let him regale them with his stories about Miriam, every one of which they believed.

After Eli was excused, they agreed that something should be done with Miriam. They didn't want such a person around their village, particularly one about whom rumors were flying. But they also had never actually punished such a person in their lifetime. Under their law, a woman taken in adultery could be stoned to death, but they had no stomach for it.

The Rabbi knew Pharisees in Jerusalem who might be able to help them resolve the problem. After consulting with them, he learned that they were very interested in helping. They were trying to entrap a wandering Rabbi by the name of Jesus. Jesus, they said, was teaching the breaking of Sabbath law. They told the Rabbi that by bringing Miriam before Jesus, they would put him to the test and show that he was truly unfaithful.

As the day after the interview passed, Miriam became more and more concerned about what was happening. The Rabbi and the elders had not spoken with her since the interview and she had no idea what it was with which they were trying to help her. Despite her shyness, she asked another neighbor if she had heard anything. The neighbor asked around and came back to Miriam, telling her that Johanna had been gossiping about her and that the Rabbi had become very upset about it. As the neighbors began to gather around Miriam and realized the gossip had been lies, they became very angry and sent a group to the Rabbi on her behalf.

"I'm sorry," the Rabbi intoned, "but this matter is now out of our hands. The Pharisees from Jerusalem now have jurisdiction and there is nothing we can do." The neighbors were furious. They went to the Pharisee the Rabbi said had taken charge. The Pharisee listened to them patiently and then tried to reassure them that Miriam would receive a fair trial.

"A trial?" the neighbors cried. "But she did nothing."

"Then she can prove she is innocent," the Pharisee replied. That further enraged the neighbors. "She doesn't have to prove her innocence," the neighbors cried. The Pharisee said, "You do not know what we know about this case. The trial will be held."

The trial was held. Rabbis were brought in to be the judges. The High Priest from the Temple presided, even though he was the one who originated the idea to test Jesus.

A Rabbi was appointed to defend Miriam. He knew that the High Priest had a vested interest and made that objection. The High Priest responded, "Be careful or we will investigate you next."

The Rabbis were not strictly traditional. After all, in Jewish court, the accusers were the prosecutors. But since Eli was a victim, he was not to be exposed to further victimization. And Johanna was a witness so she was not asked to prosecute. The Rabbis were trying to do things better than were prescribed by the Law. In addition, they also liked Jesus' teaching on adultery. Jesus had also shown that not only was there physical sin enacted in adultery, but there was also psychological sin just in the act of lust. There was no need for physical contact for there to be a punishable sin.

Johanna was called to testify and could say only what Eli had told her. The Rabbis listened intently. With great emotion, she did add that she had actually seen Eli get a hug from "that woman."

The neighbors also testified, saying that they had never seen anything unseemly and that Johanna was a gossip and that Eli was not to be trusted. Eli was never called to testify. Someone reported that he had left and wouldn't have come even if he had been called.

Miriam, her defender, and the neighbors all felt good about how the trial had gone. But the Rabbis stayed out a very long time deliberating about the case. The Rabbis finally came in. The verdict was announced. "Guilty," they said. The neighbors descended upon them and asked why they ruled that way. One Rabbi said he thought Miriam had been indiscreet about seeing Eli. Another disagreed. He said it was because Miriam had said, "Eli was a love." Another said that neither was a factor. He felt that Miriam had not proved her case. The Rabbis then got into a squabble about why they thought she was guilty. The High Priest ended the noise by declaring the verdict had been reached. He also declared that since Jesus' ideas had been considered during the trial, that he should be given a chance to respond to the declaration of guilt.

They found Jesus teaching at the Temple and took Miriam and threw her at his feet. "Tell us, Master, what we are to do with this woman found in adultery," the Pharisees said to him. The challenge was clear. If Jesus said they should not stone her, he was violating the law of Moses. If he said they had to stone her, he would lose credibility with the people who had been flocking to him.

Jesus was angered by the Pharisees. While it was common for a Rabbi to be asked to judge a case like a small claims court, he was not going to be given the chance to question the woman. It was apparent she had already faced the Rabbis' judgment. He was furious at the obvious trap.

Without looking up at the Pharisees and Rabbis, he began to write in the sand. "Abba," he wrote. "You shall love your neighbor as yourself," he wrote. And "You shall not stand forth against the life of your neighbor."

Jesus looked up at the men and said, "Moses' law says that she should be stoned. Let him among you who is without sin cast the first stone." He kneeled and wrote again in the sand, "A single witness shall not prevail against a person for any crime."

An older Rabbi slipped away.

Jesus used his finger to write in the sand, "Do unto others as you would have them do unto you."

There was the sound of shuffling of feet. Several more Rabbis and Pharisees shrugged and walked away.

At their feet, the remaining elders saw Jesus write, "Judge not, lest you be judged by your own judgment."

There was more shuffling of feet and after a few more moments, no one was there to throw the first stone. Jesus and Miriam were left without a judge to further test them.

Jesus took her by the hand and raised her up. He said, "Your accusers were wise enough to leave. How can I condemn you when they no longer do? If you sinned, don't. You be wise, too."

Miriam was wise. She discovered her real friends and, though still the quite unassuming person she was, spent time cultivating those friendships. She never saw Eli again. He did not return to the village. She did not speak with Johanna. But Johanna gave her no opportunity. For Johanna now was the friend of the Rabbi and the ten elders of the synagogue and did not deign to be with those less important.

The incident passed into the history of the village but no one there claimed it. Were it not retold by the followers of Jesus, the whole incident would have been forgotten. But the followers of Jesus would not forget justice being done.

Comment: Sometimes you can prepare a story sermon which reflects a lot of your own experience. And it becomes natural for you to play yourself while making the point of the sermon.

The following reflected a lot of my experiences as a young father. Fortunately, my wife did not die, as does the wife of the main character here. But I was quite a disappointment to my colleagues because of how much part I took in household matters and child care.

As of this writing, I am the wife my spouse always wanted! I forgot myself the other morning and illustrated a point about doing something because it needed to be done, even if my heart wasn't in it. I spoke of making breakfast and packing lunch for my wife. One of the women in the Bible study class blurted out, "Where have I gone wrong?" The men all looked away ...

You could interview a young father in your church to get his recollections about his children that enliven and instruct him and reconstruct the sermon with that material, perhaps letting him read/ tell it.

ChildREN
MATThEW 18:1-20

I was on my way to Jerusalem for the Passover. I, my father and brothers before me, my grandfather and uncles, all the men of my family have made the annual trip to the Temple since the beginning of time. This time, I had Birdie on my back. That's my daughter. A year ago, as she was being born, my wife died.

I'm sorry. I find it hard to continue.

This is Birdie's first trip to Jerusalem. She watches everything as we walk with the other pilgrims. And they watch her. There are very few women among the travelers. Someone has to stay home and tend to the children, the chores, the gardens, even the flocks in some cases. But the men must go to the Temple as part of our religious obligation.

Since my wife died, Birdie has gone everywhere with me. I take her to my little shop. I take her to the market. I take her to the well. I take her to the gate with the men. At least in my village, the men are patient with me. They presume I will marry and will then not have to bring her with me. So they never say anything. Now that she is nearly a year old, they may say something. But not so far.

Here on the road, though, there is no such patience. I hear comments like, "That's women's work," and "A real man does not take care of babies." Or, with a silly grin, someone will ask me if I plan to be married. Sometimes I think they don't think I like women and sometimes I think they want to pawn off a grouchy sister or daughter on me.

Why don't they just treat me normally? Why do they have to think they have to say something funny or say something that is thoughtless and very cutting?

A few days ago, I heard a sermon by a man named Jesus. It seems he was being accosted by some of his own friends about who is the greatest in the Kingdom of God. Jesus stopped under a tree and began to speak to them. A lot of us pilgrims gathered around. It was a nice break in the long walk and Jesus usually had something to say we could be interested in.

"Who is the greatest in the Kingdom of Heaven?" we could hear him saying as he waited for his students to gather. I was far enough away that I could not see what he was doing, but I could hear and I could feel the hot sun.

"This child is as great as any of you, and perhaps greater, for unless you are childlike, you won't even get into the Kingdom!"

The men around me murmured. I couldn't make out what they were saying. Jesus went on and everyone quieted down to listen again.

"Cherish these little ones. Don't do anything that would harm them or cause them to sin. You do, and you 'better take a flying leap' or 'go jump in the lake' because you couldn't be doing a worse thing than bringing temptation before children. If your hand or foot hurt a child, you are better off cutting it off and going into God's kingdom lame than to be whole and go to Hell."

Strong words. "Children are our futures, our social security, our pride," one old-timer groused, "but there are always more where they came from." Another said, "None of my kids were worth anything." They again quieted down as Jesus resumed speaking.

"Don't look down on children. Their angels are always surrounding the throne of God."

"And I'll bet they're underfoot up there, too!" one pilgrim wisecracked. The men around me laughed. Jesus shot a sharp glance in our direction. Then he concluded.

"You know about sheep-herding. If you have 100 sheep and one morning you wake up to find a lamb missing, you leave the 99 and hunt until you find out what happened to that lamb. If you are that good with animals, you surely can understand how God is about children. The last thing in the world God wants is to have anything bad happen to children."

"He can talk big," the smart-mouth near me mumbled. "He doesn't have any kids of his own. What does he know about children?" There were nods of approval among the other men around me.

Jesus stopped his little sermon and headed on down the road. As we got moving again, the men around me dredged up every bad story about a crazy, mean, or willful thing they had ever heard of a child doing. I was glad Birdie was too little to understand what they were talking about. And I wasn't sure I wanted to even have her hear their tone of voice. But the crowd was so thick I really had no place to go to get away from them at that point.

Birdie is the sweetest thing. As we walk along, she sometimes puts her little hands up on my neck. It is such a soft touch. The sun can't melt me like her gentle hands can. And she gurgles gladly when a new sound comes to us. There is nothing that keeps me more interested in life than seeing her interest in some new thing she's never seen, like an olive on a tree, or a peg holding two pieces of wood together.

I know she is only about a year old and can't do much, not like the neighborhood kids who sometimes sass and do mean things. But I've seen their parents be mean to them and be pretty nasty sometimes to us neighbors. Even those bad kids are good some of the time. One little girl has come over several times to help me with Birdie while I fixed supper.

Birdie does cry a lot. I wish I knew why. Sometimes I know it's that she's hungry. Sometimes she seems just to want to have a little vocal exercise. Sometimes she has a fever or a rash. But once in a while, there doesn't seem to be anything I can do to calm her down. Maybe I'm dumb, but I've done the best that I can.

Maybe I'll need to put a leash on her eventually. She doesn't wiggle around that much just yet, but she'll be walking soon. And she already reaches out to anything that looks shiny and interesting. As she matures and gets more of a mind of her own, I'm sure she's going to get into some bad things.

But the men are wrong. They seem to put all children into the same sack and think they are all alike. Pull one out and it'll make a mess. Pull out another and it'll cry. Pull out another, and it'll tip over your cup. Birdie is just herself. She isn't always going to do something bad. Those guys are wrong.

Now I'm getting upset. It's hard to be alone. I really miss ...

Sometimes I invite people over for a meal so I can have some adult company. It was so funny. One time, I had the retired Rabbi over. He never married and had not been around children, very small children, for a very long, long time. As we were eating, Birdie's little face turned quite a bright red-purple color for a few moments, smiled, and then had that "who, me?" look on her face. I was downwind. As I grabbed my innocent-looking child and left the table for a minute with her, I apologized from the other room, and got back to the meal as quickly as I could. The old Rabbi had a word for me, "My, she's a lively child." I was lucky I seated my guest upwind of Birdie!

I've called her Birdie. Her name is really Ruth. When Ruthie was about four months old, she began to eat with a lot of gusto. The moment I had put some food in her mouth, she swallowed and had her mouth open again. She was so consistent about it that she looked like a baby bird, and I've called her that ever since.

She likes music. Any time she hears anything musical, a number of bells on passing donkeys or camels, or singing, or instruments being played by musicians going by, she crawls or rolls over to the window or doorway to listen. Even though she is still less than a year old, I swear she can sing some of the tones right on pitch!

I mentioned that Birdie always sat at a meal with her mouth open. One evening, I was feeding her, as usual. Suddenly, her mouth closed tight. She wouldn't open it. I know she was still hungry. She had only eaten half of her food. Mouth closed, but her eyes bright and happy, she refused my coaxing. "You like figs," I said, trying to slip the spoon through her tightly closed lips. I pulled the spoon away, and she made a huge smile! When I put the food back near her mouth, she opened wide. Now that was at six months old! Isn't she something? I've laughed over that memory so many times.

Birdie means a lot to me.

Before my wife died, she told the midwife she hoped I would have the baby blessed by a Rabbi on its first birthday. That's today. I've been in this crowd of pilgrims now for a week, and I have sometimes been within a few yards of the Rabbi Jesus. I keep hoping for a chance to get close enough to actually speak to him.

But it hasn't happened. So I decided to push through and see if he would bless my daughter. Every time I got anywhere near him, one of his students would tell me he was busy or he was tired or he was not interested in every little request that came his way.

The last time I went near, his closest students stopped me. "The Master mustn't be disturbed," they said.

I tried to explain that I had promised, in the name of my dead wife, that I would have a Rabbi bless my daughter on her first birthday, which was today.

"Listen, my friend," a big, burly man who smelled a little like fish said, "You are being selfish to expect the Master to pay attention to you in the midst of this crowd. Your wife would certainly understand."

I stood there, terribly disappointed that he wouldn't show me any consideration, and feeling guilty that I was being so demanding. As I stood there with these mixed feelings, the crowd saw Jesus stand and so it began to move south. My moment had passed. So I thought.

There was a ruckus over near Jesus. One of his students came over to me through the crowd.

"The Master has asked me to invite you to him," he said. He grabbed my arm and pulled me through the people until we stood next to Jesus.

Birdie began to cry. He took her from my carrying sack, held her close, and then, when she didn't stop crying, tried to burp her.

"I apologize for my student's zealous desire to protect me. Your daughter's first birthday? I am honored to be the rabbi to bless her today," he said over the noise of the crowd and over the sound of Birdie crying.

It wasn't a scream or anything, just a sad-sounding but consistent crying.

Jesus tucked her in his left arm, touched her gently on the head and uttered a quiet blessing.

And Birdie just cried.

"She is a fine child and will be a comfort in your old age," Jesus said. "And she is now. Love her," he added.

My daughter cried the whole time. I was embarrassed. But Jesus wasn't.

Birdie is quiet now. Her nose began running soon after I took her back. I checked and she has two new teeth pushing through her little gums. She's sleeping now.

If anyone ever teases me again about taking care of my daughter and carting her around with me, I won't let it bother me.

My child is one of my teachers, and I don't want to miss any of God's lessons for me.

Comment: A month before, I had told this story at the church I was serving. A colleague at the Hispanic church in town invited me over to preach. I had embarrassed myself the year before by reading both the English and the Spanish versions of a sermon for them, so I decided to go with a translator this time. I sent her a triple-spaced copy of the text so she could get ready for the task.

She came prepared. While I read the story, she translated spontaneously. Even I was more captivated with her rendition, which I really did not understand, than I was with my own! I'm sorry I didn't tape record her translation for you.

I offer this story because it is done with a time dimension only lightly experimented with in the earlier stories.

ZACCHAEUS
LUKE 19:1-10

Bible stories are stories to be told, not just to be talked about.
Today, I want to tell the story of Zacchaeus, the small tax collector
who climbed a tree to see Jesus. I'm going to tell it as if I were his
son and had seen the whole thing myself. I will be telling the story
as if it happened forty years ago. That way, I can add some other
details history says about Zacchaeus that you might find interesting.

I was only a little kid when Jesus had supper with us. Actually,
he had supper with us many times. But before I get into that, let me
tell you what my dad was like.

First of all, he was not a crook. He was very honest. He pur-
chased the right to collect taxes, a proper business deal. He always
saw to it that the Roman government got what it asked for, and he
did not overcharge or threaten anyone. In fact, many times he "carried" people, mainly the farmers, paying their taxes for them until
they could pay him back.

And he was not a traitor. He was the son of a rabbi, a Jewish
teacher, and really cared about his people and his community. He
bought the right to collect taxes so he could keep other tax collectors from gouging his neighbors. He did so well that the Romans
promoted him to be chief tax collector for the region. Usually, the
Romans picked only Romans for such an important position. But
my dad was a Jew.

This was a good territory. The farm land was rich and produc-
tive, and the town of Jericho was on the main trade route to the
east. One of the reasons the Romans wanted him was because he
was so honest. He fired any of the tax collectors who worked under him if they ever cheated.

Not everyone appreciated my dad. The revolutionaries harassed
him and his workers. They called him a traitor. They even showed

people how to cheat him, which was allowed under Jewish law at the time.

At the synagogue, the rabbi did not like him. My dad still went every day. Because he contributed so well, the rabbi didn't say anything. But more than once, the rabbi called off the daily worship to spite my dad. To have daily worship at the synagogue, there have to be ten men present. If my dad was the tenth man, and no others came, the rabbi would call off worship. The rabbi felt tax collectors were the same as robbers and therefore were not really men.

Despite that, my father stuck with his religion. Let me tell you what kind of a man he was. Before he went to synagogue on the Sabbath, he showed me how he prepared his offering. He always took me to the bathroom before we left. He made sure we were in bed the night before so we would be well-rested. And he never forced me to go. He only said he had promised never to miss and then he would add how proud it made him when I went along.

Before the service started, he always went over what was going to happen, especially if there was a change. He gave me suggestions about what to do during silent prayer and helped me understand anything new that was going on if the rabbi did it differently. If I ever got to squirming, he would ask me to be patient and say that he would talk to me after the service. And he always did. One time he said he was getting bored, too, but that rabbis had bad days once in a while. That's why we should be polite and quiet.

He never passed things over my head, but let me handle the things like a grown-up. He talked to the other children that came to synagogue. And he always let me know he was glad I was there by giving me a big hug.[1]

When I was little, I thought he was the richest man in the world. Jericho was a new town, rebuilt by King Herod the Great to be his winter capital city. We had a beautiful house, a pool, a garden, and trees. We had trees!

To tell you more about my dad, Zacchaeus, I want to share one incident that happened when I was eight years old.[2] In the neighborhood there was a bad kid. He was a bully. He was nasty. He always had to have his way. But we still played with him —

73

because he had everything. If there was a new toy from India, he had it. If there was a new game from Africa, he had it. One day when I was at his house, I asked him how he got everything he wanted.

"It's easy," he said. "First, if your parents say 'no,' you stomp your feet and wave your arms. If they don't give in, then you cry and scream like you will never stop until you die. That always gets them," he told me.

Well, I decided to try it on my dad. I don't even remember what I was asked for, but when he said "no," I started stomping my feet and waving my arms. He went over to the wall and took down his flute and began playing to the rhythm of my stomping. When I slowed down, he slowed down. When I speeded up, so did he.

So I tried crying and screaming like I was never going to stop. He picked me up, carried me to my room, and said to practice crying for another hour because it was good for my lungs!

The bad kid had everything ... except my dad.

I don't remember the first time my dad had Jesus over for supper. My dad was a great one for having the visiting rabbis in for a meal and conversation. Every holiday, when the Jewish men were supposed to go up to Jerusalem for services at the Temple, my dad kept his eyes open for the rabbis who traveled through Jericho. One of his favorites was Jesus. He was one of the few who was willing to accept the invitation of a tax collector. It was no big deal until Jesus got famous.

This one year, when Jesus was heading south to celebrate the Passover, the crowds were huge. My dad heard by the grapevine that Jesus was coming through town. When he went out to see his friend, the crowd was so big he could not get near him. Now my dad was not presumptuous, nor was he very tall. So he climbed up in a tree to at least have a look at Jesus, and to wave to his friend as he went by.

Well, Jesus saw him and invited himself to supper.

The next day, the rabbi at our synagogue denounced Jesus for eating with tax collectors and sinners. The day after that, the revolutionaries killed two of my dad's workers and tried to make it look like bandits had done it. My dad called all of his workers in for their safety and kept us at home.

We heard later that Jesus had proceeded to Jerusalem, chased the cheaters out of the Temple, and a week later, was put on trial and executed.

It was a very bad time for us. Tensions were very high. We all stayed home for weeks, skipping the trip to Jerusalem we should have taken for Passover. At Pentecost, we decided to risk it and went to Jerusalem as we were supposed to.

While we were there, Dad heard a man named Peter preach about Jesus. That day, he joined Peter's group. He committed all his income to the group there in Jerusalem. We went back home to Jericho where Dad worked. Living off our savings, we kept our home and his job so that his income could help the Jesus-followers.

Things went well for several years that way. As the Church developed and spread, my dad's income supported about two dozen people to be full-time preachers, teachers, and missionaries.

Occasionally, one of the emperors or governors would blame Christians for all the world's problems. Things would get rough. People would disappear and not be seen again. Or their bodies would appear at a particular stone pile outside of town.

They didn't touch my dad, because he continued to collect taxes. The revolutionaries apparently decided to let him alone because he was fair, even after they had killed his workers.

I was about 35, and living in Antioch, when I heard that my parents had disappeared.

I don't know what happened to them. One rumor is that they were in prison in Caesarea where Paul the apostle was jailed. The rumor went on that, after he was released, my dad became the leader of the church there.

There are a lot of stories about my dad, Zacchaeus. I'll never forget him. When things get really tough, I will always remember my dad saying, "Whenever you are feeling down and worthless, remember Jesus had supper with us!"

Every time I eat now, I think of how Jesus came to us at supper, even the family of a tax collector. Remember, he comes to you, too.

1. This list of parent-child activities was included in a friend's church newsletter, now long residing in a circular file.

2. My recollection is that this story was told by Garrison Keillor.

Comment: Before I got started telling story sermons and dramatizing Bible stories at the church I was serving, I was invited to take part in a Good Friday ecumenical service. Instead of the Seven Last Words, we were asked to preach on the "Seven Other Words." I was assigned "Jesus of Nazareth, King of the Jews."

At the time, our city had a rash of police brutality incidents. One in particular had caused a great uproar in the city. A young African-American man stopped to see if he could help at the scene of an accident. As he was returning to his car, a police officer grabbed him and accused him of robbing a nearby store. He protested his innocence to no avail. In anger, he struggled to free himself of the officer's grasp. The officer then put a neck hold on him that rendered the young man unconscious. He was dragged to the police van. Another officer noticed the young man had stopped breathing but did nothing about it. The young man died.

As I wrote this, living in another city several years later, a similar death had occurred.

As I thought about that horrifying incident and about the sign over Jesus' head as he hung on the cross, I started "hearing" a conversation in my imagination between two men in the crowd watching the crucifixion. My notes for the conversation put the visitor's statements on the left side of the paper. The "local" man's responses and narrative were on the right. When I preached the sermon, I leaned to the left when I "talked" the notes on the visitor. And I leaned to the right as I did the local man's lines.

For this book, I have put the text into more standard dialogue.

Pilate's Sign
John 19:19-22

Introduction: The crowd that had followed the soldiers and Jesus was now just standing around watching and waiting. The nails had been pounded into Jesus' hands and feet. The cross had been raised and pounded down into its hole. The initial shock upon the onlookers of the scream of pain had worn off. In fact, it was quiet as those watching waited to see Jesus and the other criminals on their crosses die.

One man, a visitor, turns to the man next to him, who apparently was from Jerusalem, a "local," to find out what was going on.

Visitor: Who is that guy in the middle?

Local: A rabbi from down north.

Visitor: What's he done?

Local: I'm not really sure.

Visitor: I can't read. What's that sign over the rabbi's head say?

Local: "Jesus of Nazareth, King of the Jews."

Visitor: What's that about?

Local: The judge has to label his handiwork with the formal accusation. Pilate is laying it on the local leaders. In three languages yet! Hebrew, Greek, and Latin.

Visitor: Who's this Pilate?

Local: He's the Roman governor. This area is on every trade route on this end of the Mediterranean. It's too important to let it run its own affairs.

Visitor: What's he do?

Local: He acts as chief judge and enforcer.

Visitor: He's the main sign of Roman power here, then.

Local: He sure thought so when he first came here. He brought in his Roman Guard. Unlike his predecessor, he did not have his

Guard remove the busts of Caesar from his flagstaffs. Romans treat their ruler as God. We Jews believe in only one God and that is NOT Caesar. The former governor respected that and didn't want to aggravate the people here. Pilate felt he had to prove how powerful he was. Jewish leaders challenged him, saying they wanted God honored, not Caesar. Pilate decided to follow the Jewish leaders back to their residence. He took his Roman Guards with him. When they got there, the Guard surrounded the leaders and threatened to attack them if they ever challenged Pilate again.

Visitor: What did the Jews do?

Local: In defiance, the Jewish leaders tore open their robes and bared their necks to the Roman Guard.

Visitor: Then what happened?

Local: Pilate backed down. He must have realized that this was no way to start off being governor here.

Visitor: Did things improve?

Local: Things quieted down for a while. Then a drought came along and water for Jerusalem became a problem. In order to dig new wells, Pilate needed money, but he wasn't ready to raise taxes in the middle of the drought. After making sure the taxes were enforced, he still needed more money, so he went to the Temple and just took as much of the Temple money as he needed. That money was the Korban, the discretionary fund held by the religious power structure made up of tithes from the Pharisees. The city rioted. Pilate had his guard change out of their uniforms into clothing like we wear. He sent them out into the crowds to get close to the ringleaders. At his signal, the Guard pulled out their swords and killed many of the people along with the leaders. Word was sent to Rome and they threatened to pull Pilate out for his rash actions.

Visitor: His job was on the line then?

Local: That's probably why he handled the trial of the rabbi the way he did. First of all, when the Temple leaders brought Jesus to Pilate, Pilate asked what the accusation was. They didn't say. They just asked Pilate if he believed they had brought him a good man. Pilate told them to take Jesus out and handle him their own way. But the leaders pointed out that they couldn't execute Jesus. Only the Romans had that authority.

Visitor: Did the leaders ever come up with an accusation? It had to be bad to want Jesus killed.

Local: They said Jesus wanted to be king.

Visitor: But Herod was already king, right?

Local: That's right. So Pilate took Jesus off to talk with him privately. One of the guards told me that Pilate asked him if he wanted to be king. Jesus asked Pilate, "Is that your opinion or just their accusation?" Pilate answered back that he didn't know. He wasn't from here. He asked Jesus what he had done. Jesus didn't deny he was king. He just wasn't the kind of king the leaders and Pilate thought. If he was, Jesus said, he'd have sent in armies to battle with the Romans. Pilate said, "You are a king then?" And Jesus told him his kingdom had to do with sharing truth about life and being. Pilate got exasperated. He shouted, "What is truth?" Here he had the power people in Rome ready to dump him and he had the Jewish people pushing him from the other side. And Jesus was talking philosophy!

Visitor: Sounds more like religion to me.

Local: Pilate maybe thought so. He brought Jesus back out and yelled at the leaders and their crowd that Jesus was clean. He asked them what their problem was.

Visitor: That should have stopped the whole thing right there.

Local: It didn't. The leaders in the crowd started chanting, "Kill him." Pilate quieted them down and yelled, "You have a custom. It's Passover. You can ask for the release of a prisoner." Pilate tried to think of the worst crook in his prisons to suggest. Even before he offered his name, the crowd began to chant, "Barabbas."

Visitor: Who's that?

Local: He was always a crook, known for theft and murder. He had been recruited by the leaders to join the Zealots to harass the Roman soldiers and the tax collectors. He got caught. It never occurred to Pilate that the crowd would prefer Barabbas to Jesus.

Visitor: That sure backfired. Is that when Pilate gave in?

Local: Pilate had another trick up his sleeve. He had his soldiers beat Jesus, put a purple robe on him and make a crown of thorns on his head. There was blood all over. But Jesus was still alive. Pilate yelled to the crowd, "Look at him!" The crowd yelled back, "Crucify him!" Then someone in the crowd yelled, "He claims he's the son of God." That surprised Pilate and threw him. He went over to Jesus and asked him, "Who are you?" Jesus didn't answer him. Pilate threatened, "I have power over you." Jesus replied, "Who gives you that power?"

Visitor: Good question!

Local: Right. Pilate knew he had the official authority, and he knew the crowd wanted it. But he wanted to refuse. He said, "Let him go." But the people in the crowd yelled back, "Whose friend are you, Pilate? Caesar's? Jesus tried to be king."

Visitor: Really? Did that really happen?

Local: A few months ago, some people cornered Jesus after he had done some healings and had been gathering large crowds. They tried to get him to become king. But he walked away from it all. He didn't want any part of being the kind of king they wanted. Maybe Pilate had heard a little about that incident. The mob had his attention with that accusation. They yelled, "Anyone trying to be king is against Caesar."

Visitor: They were really pushing Pilate's buttons, weren't they?

Local: He was so mad, he cleared everyone back, jumped down from his judgment seat, had the soldiers put Jesus in his chair, and yelled, "Here is your king!" But the crowd yelled, "Crucify him!" "Shall I crucify your king?" The crowd yelled back, "WE HAVE NO KING BUT CAESAR!"

Visitor: They yelled what?

Local: "We have no king but Caesar." That blew Pilate away. He knew how strongly even we feel that Caesar is not our king. God is. After they had bared their necks just over the busts of Caesar on the flag staffs, he knew they were crazy now.

Visitor: That's when he gave up?

Local: Yeah. He handed Jesus over to the soldiers and ordered he be crucified.

Visitor: That's why the sign?

Local: He had to put something up there.

Visitor: I'll bet that ticked off the leaders.

Local: Believe it. They wanted him to write "He said he was King ..." But Pilate got in their faces and said, "I have written what I have written." The leaders got what they wanted, Jesus eliminated. And Pilate got what he wanted, a symbolic victory.

Visitor: A what?

Local: A symbolic victory. That's like when you score a basket with two seconds left but you still lost by twenty points.

Visitor: Pilate didn't lose. Jesus did ... Could Pilate have really won?

Local: Yes, he could have stayed in the judgment seat and declared Jesus innocent.

Visitor: But why didn't he?

Local: Forgot he had the power? Personality conflicts with his bosses and with the leaders here?

Visitor: Maybe he just had a bad day?

Local: Maybe he figured the leaders were more to blame than he was.

Visitor: But he wasn't Jesus.

Local: But he wasn't Jesus. What's another human being so long as it wasn't himself?

Visitor: I'll bet Pilate never walked a mile in another man's shoes. I guess he's not so different from us. I heard the police let someone die without helping him because he tried to escape. They didn't pay attention when he stopped breathing. We get very callous, don't we?

Local: Long as it isn't us in custody, or getting beat on, I guess we let some terrible things happen.

Visitor: What's that guy Jesus yelling?

Local: "Father, forgive them, for they know not what they are doing."

Comment: I am a Sherlock Holmes* fan. In early 1983, I got to wondering what would happen if Sherlock Holmes investigated the Resurrection. On Good Friday evening, I decided to go to work on a short, short story to be used the Sunday after Easter during a congregational hymn sing. I already had a sermon started for Easter Sunday.

As I began to write, I heard the voices and literally let the story flow from what I was hearing. After working two hours I had two problems. One, the story was already a page longer than my original goal for length, and I wasn't halfway through the story. Two, I didn't have the foggiest idea how the story was going to come out!

It was a restless night, though no story elements worked their way to the surface as I tossed and turned. I was facing a pressure-filled circumstance in the weeks to come and had no room in my consciousness for creativity.

The next morning, I drove myself to finish tasks I had to get done so that I could get back to the Holmes story. I wanted to know what was going to happen next! I worked four hours on it that afternoon. And the ending surprised me!

I used the story for my Easter sermon, I liked it so much. In reading it at the Easter service, I even tried to use accents from the British Isles for some of the characters. Unfortunately, I could not satisfy my ear for Holmes and Watson. And I did not have it in shape for use by members of the congregation, something that could be done fairly easily, given more time.

If you try your hand at this premise, your effort could be very different from mine. I would certainly not be surprised or hurt! I have already had my reward, having the story happen to me, like listening to Dr. Watson himself tell it!

*Sherlock Holmes and Dr. Watson were created by Sir Arthur Conan Doyle.

The Adventure Of The Empty Tomb
Mark 16:1-8

One would expect a day in late March to be dreary in London, but this was a gem. We could see the top of the Cathedral fully four miles away from our digs at 221B Baker Street. Rarely is the air so clear, and on this particular day, so warm in the early spring. It was Good Friday.

My friend, Sherlock Holmes, was not religious in the traditional sense, and, though I attended services of a Sunday as a rule, I seldom attended the extra services surrounding holidays.

"It is a marvel to see the Cathedral from here," Holmes remarked as he took in the loveliness of the day. "You don't suppose God is trying to tell me something," he said with a cheerful smile. No pietist, he, nor ordinarily concerned with theological matters, he occasionally astonished me with his awareness of things religious.

"I dare say the gentleman coming from the carriage to our door is a clergyman of some high post," Holmes observed.

I joined him at the window and saw an elderly, well-dressed gentleman, quite unassuming in appearance.

"How do you know he's from the church?" I asked.

"Elementary. I have seen the man conduct services at the Cathedral!"

Ordinarily, Holmes deduces a great deal from items of apparel, jewelry, and other visible things. Indeed, I would have laughed were it not for the worried look upon the good Anglican priest's face as he glanced up toward our window.

Mrs. Hudson ushered him in momentarily, and Holmes, in his accustomed fashion, graciously seated him and put his cloak and cane in the closet.

"Your worship, this is my friend, Dr. John Watson, emanuensis of my trifling adventures. Whatever your concern, I'm certain you may trust his discretion."

"Grace and peace to you both," our elderly guest began. "Mr. Holmes, I am fully aware of your agnosticism regarding matters of belief. I may be imposing, but I am desperate for an unusual kind of help."

"Pray tell us what concerns you. We will be of help in any way we can."

"Oh, Mr. Holmes, can you prove the resurrection of our Lord Jesus Christ?" the priest blurted out.

"That is an astonishing task to which you would put me," Holmes replied, raising his voice a little. "What causes this matter of faith to become so specific an historical concern to you?"

"There are always those laity who strike out at the Church for some real or imagined wrong they believe the Church has perpetrated against them," the priest began. "They pick up on such as Saint Matthew gives in his gospel about the soldiers telling the city folk the disciples stole the body. We are accustomed to such attacks. They rarely cause a ripple in the Church. However, a very different matter has come to my attention and it bodes ill for the Church. The Archbishop of Canterbury himself has become extremely depressed of late. His homilies have become more and more gloomy."

"A nervous breakdown, perhaps," I suggested.

"Perhaps, Dr. Watson," he replied, "but it has none of the typical antecedents of overwork and ill health. This year has been especially good for the Archbishop. There have been few personnel or financial difficulties, and relationships with the Methodists and the Romans have been amicable. His being celibate, there are none of the marital difficulties that often accompany or even cause such a condition. No, we are quite sure he is not mentally ill."

"There are tumors that disorient a person or change a personality," I further volunteered.

"But there are no headaches and no motor dysfunctions, my good doctor. He is well-coordinated and suffers naught," the clergyman pointed out.

"Is there a genesis for his symptoms, a time when something important occurred that may be causing so sad a set of symptoms?" Holmes inquired.

"He has been loath to address his languor or our concern. But on one occasion he mentioned something about a time device of some sort."

"A clock? How odd," I opined.

"Oh, no. Dr. Watson, a device that moves people through time. H. G. Wells has come upon such a device and shared his discovery with the Archbishop. The Archbishop has not been the same since. But he has given no further clues to help us help him."

"I've heard of such a device. It would appear that the Archbishop may have been duped by Dr. Wells," Holmes remarked.

"We thought of that, too, Mr. Holmes. But upon inquiring, we heard denials from Dr. Wells and, indeed, found him to be most open and obviously concerned."

"This is most peculiar. I have an idea how we might help. This is a serious day for you, so we shall take no more of your time, Your Grace. We will be in touch," Holmes said as he retrieved the cane and cloak belonging to his guest.

"Much obliged," the reverend said, "and God bless you, Mr. Holmes."

They bowed respectfully toward one another and the clergyman was gone.

"All the credible are not possible, thus leaving only the incredible remaining to be true. Watson, it appears there is to be a most peculiar journey ahead."

There was indeed. We had some difficulty working our way to the laboratory of Dr. Wells because there were only a few carriages available due to the holy day. And then we hit a fanatic who would only allow a fare to go a mile at which point he would stand and claim to ride further would be work on a holy day. Holmes' effort to resolve the mystery of the Resurrection had an awkward beginning.

We attained the Wells residence after considerable walking. He ushered us in, almost as though we were expected.

"I must admit I have been worried about the Archbishop. He was most upset when he returned," Dr. Wells shared with us.

"He apparently happened upon evidence that the Resurrection did not occur," Holmes suggested.

"So it would seem, Mr. Holmes," Dr. Wells replied. "Not having gone along, I could not begin to say what he found."

"May I have the privilege of a journey in your time vehicle, sir?" my friend asked.

"Of course, Mr. Holmes. I will prepare the machine."

"Tomorrow, Dr. Wells?" Holmes proposed.

"That will be fine. About 11 a.m. then?" Dr. Wells offered.

With a nod, Holmes accepted and went to the door.

"Come along. Watson, We have much homework to do."

He spent the early evening poring over the Gospel stories of the Resurrection, studying maps of Jerusalem and surrounding territories, and anything else he could find in his amazing library. And then he sat until the wee hours of the morning, pondering the matter midst a heavy haze of smoke from his shag.

He was still worried when we made our way to Dr. Wells' laboratory. He and Dr. Wells spoke at length in low tones. Then Holmes thoroughly examined the time machine inside and out.

"There still is a matter that concerns me greatly. I am fluent in Norwegian, French, and German, but there was no time to study Middle Eastern languages last night. What was the Archbishop's experience?" Holmes inquired.

"He spoke not of it, Mr. Holmes," Dr. Wells replied, "but he did not complain either."

"Then let me be off," Holmes responded. He climbed into the contraption. It began to vibrate and then to shake rather violently. I became alarmed and rushed toward it to help my friend when it suddenly stopped. Holmes jumped out safely, thank goodness.

"Thank you, Doctor. Come Watson, we must now interview the Archbishop," he said as he strode rapidly toward the door.

He was silent as we rode to the Cathedral. It being Saturday, the streets were not busy. The fine weather held and there were hopes that Easter would be celebrated in such a sunny condition.

The Archbishop was sitting in his office. His drapes were drawn and the bright sun barely crept through the folds to dimly illumine the ornate room. Around him were books, papers, and a supply of pens and ink. But none of the books were opened, and there was not a mark upon the papers.

His training as a gentleman slowly brought him to his feet as we were ushered in by his assistant, the clergyman who had come to us the day before. The Archbishop's face was grave, careworn, and there was as little life in his eyes as there was light in the room. He said nothing.

"Thank you for allowing me this interview, Your Grace," Holmes greeted him. We took seats next to his desk and Holmes went right to his subject.

"I was there, too," he said.

"Holmes, you what?" I fairly shouted. "You never left that infernal machine!"

"Watson, Watson, it is a time machine, and it was set to return me barely a moment after I left. I was there for the better part of twenty hours. And I believe it will help the Archbishop to report my perambulations and studies."

For the first time, the eyes of the Archbishop focussed intently on my friend, waiting, and, it appeared, hoping.

"Your grace, let me pass over the Resurrection. The boy is alive."

"He's ... alive? But how? How did you...?" stammered the patriarch.

"I know that faith is usually able to fill in around the absence of facts or even contradiction in facts; and the Gospels are replete with both when it comes to the Resurrection stories. One angel or two in the tomb or none? Could Jesus be touched or could he not? To whom did he first appear?"

"No exegetical theology, please, Mr. Holmes, tell me about the boy." The Archbishop was on his feet imploring my companion, life returning to his eyes, tempered by the dread that Holmes might not be on the mark.

"I was able to move him before you arrived. It was difficult to communicate the danger, but I was able to entice him away from where you landed by a little string magic my grandmother taught me when I was a child. Dr. Wells told me when and where you landed when you returned to the time of Christ. I examined the vehicle and found traces of blood and hair on one corner, and surmised a dreadful accident had occurred. So we reset the device to get me there before you and with enough time for me to save the boy."

"Where did you set down? Jerusalem was so crowded that even the rock called Golgotha where I landed had pilgrims camping upon it."

"I chose the Valley of Hinnom. Although there were many poor, deformed souls in the garbage heaps of Jerusalem, there are places on the slopes that I felt the machine could land safely. We succeeded in hitting a level spot, but as Watson here will attest, it was quite unstable and was a most shaky landing. I made my way to Golgotha in plenty of time and found the boy."

"Oh, Mr. Holmes! Oh, Mr. Holmes! You can't know the relief I feel! How could anyone have understood my guilt? It had never occurred to me that I could cause so grievous a death, fulfilling an ego trip like that. I was so stricken, I could not even speak to Dr. Wells when I returned. Oh, Mr. Holmes ... My, but it is dark in here. Let me open the drapes!"

The old man fairly sprang from his place next to my companion to give the sun a chance to pour in. It was as if he had been raised from the dead!

Before us, back on Baker Street, sat a marvelous lamb stew Mrs. Hudson had prepared for us for our evening meal. Holmes pounced upon it with delight. He had enjoyed the sunny ride back from the Cathedral as had I. But now my curiosity built up and I desired to ascertain what else he'd done during the time he was there.

"Yes, Watson, I'll tell you," he said in response to my query.

"Arriving well before the Archbishop did, I set out to be sure I found the proper tomb. I could have followed the Archbishop, but I chose to investigate on my own. There are two tombs, according to scholars, that seem to have been where Jesus of Nazareth could have been buried. I went to both to be sure I knew which it was. The one beneath Golgotha had a small troop of Roman guards. The other did not, so I decided the first had to be it.

"Just before the Archbishop was due to arrive, I went and found the boy and removed him from danger.

"Very early the next morning, before sunup, I made my way to the tomb. To my surprise, there was no Roman guard. I thought I had made a mistake, but I was not about to try to get to the other tomb. I took my chances and decided to have a closer look. The stone was still over the opening to the tomb. I rolled it back. It was a most difficult struggle, but Mrs. Hudson's good meals fueled my effort.

"The eastern sky was by now fairly light and I felt it would allow me to see inside. The tomb was empty.

"Just then, the women came out. The first ray of the sun came through the entrance and struck me. It startled the women so that they turned and ran.

"By the light I now had, I could see the cloths left behind. They had been neatly folded. Just then, I heard the Archbishop approach, so I stepped back into the shadows. The women, having regained their composure, returned. They seemed to see us both. This time, they did not run.

"The Archbishop, knowing Aramaic, told them Jesus was gone, and that they would see him in Galilee."

"But how do you suppose the Archbishop was able to come, having thought he'd killed the boy?" I asked.

"My dear Watson, he had come in well into the evening when it was dark and there was little movement among the campers. He did not realize the vehicle had struck the boy. He found the child crushed beneath it when he returned after his visit to the tomb. I'm sure he attempted to help the child but may have had to flee in the time vehicle when the people misunderstood and threatened him."

"What happened to the Roman guard?" I wondered.

"It seems there was a mix-up and the overnight assignment was not taken. The guard appeared after the women and the Archbishop had left. I was outside examining the ground for signs of the presence of others who might have come in the night to steal the body of Jesus. I hid myself when the soldiers appeared, so they did not see me. They were quite angry to find no guard, to find the tomb opened, and to find it empty. My smattering of Italian helped me understand they worked out a story about an angel putting its muscle upon them. They left hastily.

"Then came two men, Peter and John, I presume, who noticed the way the grave cloths lay. They, too, left hurriedly.

"I waited in the shrubbery, expecting Mary Magdalene any moment. The wait was fruitful in a remarkable way. She was a very striking woman. She almost made me forget Irene Adler!

"As I watched, a man I had not seen before came and spoke with her. He was simply clothed and ordinary looking. But Mary, if my recollection of the Gospel of John is correct, apparently took him to be Jesus and she fell on her knees. He spoke briefly to her. She rose and hastened away.

"The man looked over toward me and beckoned to me. He met me halfway."

"Holmes, was it ... was it ... Jesus?" I blurted out.

"When I spoke to him, he didn't understand my words, and I could not decipher his. I looked quickly for wounds, but his sandals covered the place on his feet through which the nails would have been driven. His hands he kept at his side and his cloak covered them. There were scratches where the crown of thorns might have been, but he could also have gotten them walking through low branches there near the tomb."

"Didn't you try to find out some way?" I urged.

"I put my hands out toward him, palms up, hoping he would do the same. He smiled, turned, and walked away."

"You followed him, of course."

"No, I was content. I needed no further evidence."

"But, Holmes ..." I persisted.

"Watson, you know the story from the Gospel of Saint Luke about the poor man, Lazarus, and the rich man, Dives?"

"Yes, I do, but what has that to do with the Resurrection of Jesus?"

"Father Abraham, with whom Lazarus was, told Dives that even if someone returned from the dead, that would not persuade anyone. As you saw with the Archbishop, what changes people is not the empty tomb, but a heart freed of guilt ..."

My friend, Sherlock Holmes, paused. Then with a twinkle in his eye, he said, "... which, quite frankly, has rarely been a problem with me."

"Oh, Holmes ..." I said, and we laughed together.

Comment: Several times over the years, I preached a series of sermons out of the letter to the Galatians. Having tried a number of other dramatic techniques, I decided to have a phone conversation between Paul and Barnabas. I prepared a script and got two phones, one for me (Barnabas is one of the great saints of the New Testament and I played him) and one for a church member who played Paul.

In succeeding weeks, I went further, having a four-way phone consultation including a representative of the Judaizing party and a regular church member, representing those caught in the middle of the controversy that swirled around Paul at that time.

For the purposes of this book, I decided to include only this one story sermon as an illustration.

I included no introduction because I had already traced the stories of both Paul and Barnabas in previous sermons of the more normal variety. And I had pulled no punches about how Paul came across (untranslatable nasty language in Galatians, for example). Fortunately, the lay person reading the Paul part was able to be nasty-sounding enough to make this work okay.

Called To Freedom
Galatians 5:1, 6, 13-15

Paul: Hello.

Barnabas: Paul, is that you? This is Barnabas.

Paul: It's me, Barnabas. What do you want?

Barnabas: Did you get my letter?

Paul: The one about how I crushed the Galatians with my anger? Yes, I got it.

Barnabas: It doesn't sound like I scored any points with you.

Paul: You missed the whole point of my letter. You were being your old, gentle, gloss-over-everything self.

Barnabas: Paul, you're not exactly the easiest guy in the world to work with, you know.

Paul: I don't have to take this. If this were my nickel, I'd hang up.

Barnabas: I hope you'll hang on instead. I need to clear up a few things with you and I'll gladly pay for it.

Paul: Whatever you say, Zeus, ol' buddy!

Barnabas: When we went through Galatia several years ago, you taught circumcision. We were challenged by people in every church there about that. And you had an answer for them, that circumcision was a reminder of our tie with Abraham and his covenant with God. It was a bodily reminder that we are a part of that covenant. Benjamin and his group are teaching essentially the same thing. How come you are so angry with them?

Paul: Which question do you want me to answer?

Barnabas: I don't understand.

Paul: I know that! You asked two things: Is there a difference between what we taught and what Benjamin teaches? That's one question. The other is: Why am I so angry? Well, Benjamin is not teaching the same thing at all. When we were there, you remember that we did not circumcise everyone. The flak we got over it was too much. You, with your accommodating ways, probably thought we should always circumcise unless it would cause hard feelings.

Barnabas: Wait a minute. It wasn't hard feelings I was worried about. It was respect for their opinion and the realization that it would take years to work around those feelings. I was being respectful and patient.

Paul: And missing the point, as usual.

Barnabas: Paul!

Paul: Listen, you want to talk or not?

Barnabas: Okay.

Paul: As I was saying, we didn't circumcise everyone. What began to sink in with me was that we were simply hanging onto a practice which was symbolic. I stopped circumcising, not because of an obstruction that would be overcome eventually, but because it wasn't crucial. It wasn't even important.

Barnabas: Wait up there! Not even important! How can you say that? You were the one who made it sound so important. That's why they reacted so strongly.

Paul: Can I help it if people take everything I say literally? You remember I only preached it. I didn't demand it.

Barnabas: Sure sounded like you demanded it.

Paul: Look, I happen to like the Abraham story very much, and I respect the way he started so many of our traditions. I still think we should encourage the traditions that help us work out our own salvation, and help us to avoid being squeezed into the world's mold. What I thought I was preaching was faithfulness to God, not the necessity of a particular ritual. I'll bet someday that followers of John the Baptist will insist that everyone have adult total immersion baptism and they'll be quoting me that I demanded it!

Barnabas: How else are we to take you?

Paul: Listen to *everything* I say, not just your pet ideas from me. I know that's confusing. I've changed my mind on some things and I've said some things people can easily take out of context. My point on circumcision was that it is a very physical celebration of our unity in Abraham and God's covenant with him. It doesn't hurt to do physical signs to help us stick by our commitments.

95

Barnabas: There you go again, telling me you're for circumcision.

Paul: No, listen to me. I am not *against* it. There are good things about it. I'll probably preach circumcision the rest of my life. But, it is not important! Do you hear that? *It is not important!*

Barnabas: But Abraham was circumcised.

Paul: When?

Barnabas: About two thousand years ago.

Paul: Barnabas, was he circumcised before or after he did his act of faith?

Barnabas: After. After he left his home in Ur.

Paul: And after he went to Mount Moriah to sacrifice Isaac.

Barnabas: I never thought of that.

Paul: What was so great about Abraham? Not that he was circumcised, but that he *trusted God!* That's the difference between Benjamin and me.

Barnabas: Now wait, Benjamin also talks about Abraham's faith in God. He says it was faith that led him to the covenant with God and to be circumcised.

Paul: That's where Benjamin and the Judaizers stop ... with circumcision.

Barnabas: No, they have everyone learn the rules of life developed around the Ten Commandments; you know, the Sabbath work laws — I mean the Sabbath non-work laws — the hygiene rules, and so forth. They even have those Gentiles celebrating Passover and the other Jewish holidays.

Paul: Hooray for Benjamin. He's got them all tied up so that they can't be free.

Barnabas: Well, we thought their problem was that they didn't have any rules for living.

Paul: The Galatians sure did! God gave them some pretty good ones in their old religions, through common sense, and through the ones we shared with them from Jesus.

Barnabas: Jesus was circumcised, baptized, Temple-ized, the whole Jewish bit.

Paul: But Jesus broke with them at this point: *It wasn't that important!*

Barnabas: Paul, you are going to make wild men out of everyone talking like that.

Paul: No, you still aren't hearing me. I'm not saying the law is bad in and of itself. It *is* a gift of God. All the Temple rules, hygiene laws, holidays, all that — they're gifts of God. *But they are not God.*

Barnabas: No one says they are.

Paul: Benjamin and his ilk say they are.

Barnabas: Come on, Paul. All they are doing is emphasizing the rituals more than we do. I don't like it either, really. I know how it is tearing up the church in Galatia.

Paul: That's the sign there is a problem. They've got everyone squabbling. When there's party spirit like that, I feel God has been pushed aside.

Barnabas: But, Paul, when you wrote to Galatia, you fanned the blaze that was burning there.

Paul: Why don't people listen to the whole message instead of picking out the little bitty parts they want to hear? Let me put it this way. There are two kinds of people, those who have faith and those who follow rules.

Barnabas: Everybody does both.

Paul: Let me finish. Those who have faith have it because they have discovered God loves them. They are like children of Abraham's real wife. Those who follow rules are like the children of Abraham's slave wife, Hagar, because they think they will be safe if they follow the rules.

Barnabas: But the children of Sara follow rules and the children of Hagar have faith.

Paul: Now we are getting to the important part. What is the faith of the children of Hagar, the children of slavery?

Barnabas: That their rules will keep them doing the will of God.

Paul: Very good. But does it?

Barnabas: Keep them within the will of God? Well ... mostly.

Paul: Very good. You and I both know the law does not cover everything. We have to interpret the law every time we turn around in order to make it fit. You know the old argument, "Is it work to do a deed of mercy on the Sabbath?" If you walk more than a mile or if you get dirty, then you violate the Sabbath. But if you don't help the ox or the man out of the ditch, you violate the law which says, "Do unto others as you would have them do unto you." The law is incomplete. And it conflicts with itself.

Barnabas: But you still haven't said what the difference is.

Paul: The law is always going to be contradictory. Sooner or later, the more laws, the more loopholes for doing what you want, either to be selfish or to harm others. At best, it is a tool, a guide, and I will grant, in some circumstances, a real gift. But *Benjamin has made it god.*

Barnabas: No, Paul, he says it is *from* God.

Paul: Answer me this question: What does he say loses us our salvation?

Barnabas: Try that with different words.

Paul: What does he say separates us from the love of God?

Barnabas: Violating the covenant.

Paul: How do we know if we have violated the covenant?

Barnabas: When we break the law.

Paul: What do we have then?

Barnabas: God angry at us.

Paul: Then what?

Barnabas: We have to get our act together and get back to obeying the law.

Paul: See?

Barnabas: I still don't see.

Paul: How do you get your act back together?

Barnabas: Well, you ... just do it.

Paul: Right ... especially when you get down on yourself about having broken the law. Easy to start over, right? Far easier to get cynical about yourself!

Barnabas: Okay, I think I understand that. What keeps us from becoming cynical about ourselves?

Paul: Two things. One, we can understand God as having sent Jesus to be the one who takes our punishment for the sins we've done, and thus offers us a reprieve. That gets some people going. The other is a word.

Barnabas: A word?

Paul: Yes, one Jesus used. "Abba."

Barnabas: You mentioned both of those in your letter. But can a word change everything so we don't get cynical?

Paul: Think about it. What is God like to you?

Barnabas: He's my father, my "abba," my daddy.

Paul: Right. What's God like to Benjamin?

Barnabas: Oooo, now I'm getting it. To him, God is pretty vengeful. God is hovering over Benjamin's shoulder watching to see if he is dotting every "i" and crossing every "t."

Paul: If the law is so important, even God becomes subject to the law and the law becomes God.

Barnabas: You lost me there.

Paul: Forget it. Just remember Abraham's faith was in "Abba" — Father. Jesus' faith was in "Abba" — Father. Yours is, too. If God is that way toward us, forgiving, giving us a chance to follow His will, then God is God and is worth our trust. *Trust,* that's a key word, too. If God is trustable, then we can put our sins behind us like He does, and go back to the business of living.

Barnabas: But doesn't that leave God open to the accusation that He doesn't care what we do?

Paul: If you trust someone, you aren't going to intentionally mess up that relationship, are you?

Barnabas: Not if I can help it. But that doesn't put a vengeful God hovering over me ... it puts a mothering God there, one I have to be careful not to hurt the feelings of.

Paul: No, not really. You know you are relaxed when you are trusted. When your folks stopped hovering over you, you became a man, right?

Barnabas: Right. Oh, I got advice from my dad and my mom when they forgot I was grown up. But I really didn't feel like an adult until I realized they trusted me, and that I had to be able to operate on my own as a human being.

Paul: They finally let you grow up. And your trust in them was based not on their hovering, but on their wisdom. And they weren't always there to provide that wisdom, so you had to make judgments on your own. You took into account what they had taught you. That's the "law." But you looked beyond specifics of what they said once in a while to do what was the patient, forgiving, caring, loving thing to do, not out of fear of your parents and what they might do to you, but because you knew that they would do the same thing if they were in your shoes. So you have acted in ways that sustain your trusting relationship with your parents.

Barnabas: But that reminds me. You haven't talked about your anger and the way it messed up your relationships with the Galatians.

Paul: I don't want to talk about it.

Barnabas: God cares what you do and if you don't get hold of yourself on that ...

Paul: Good-bye.

Barnabas: Paul? Paul? Well, you don't need to be that angry! Paul? Guess he'd rather talk to the cat.[1] I'll call him back next week.

---

1. Garrison Keillor told a story at the time about someone who enjoyed talking with his cat more than with people ... Puff never talked back!

Comment: Hostages had been part of everyday news for all of the decade of the 1980s. It seemed appropriate to look back into the scriptures to see if there were any materials that might have meaning in that kind of historical context.

While Paul was not a hostage in the classic sense, he was under house arrest a number of times, thus separated from his family and friends, and from his task as ambassador for Christ. I decided to drop the hostage notion and just concentrate on the way things were for the story line. Storytelling can do that to you, give you a premise and then take it away, and still come up with something you feel is worth working on.

It was not hard, once I examined the letter to the Philippians, to imagine a satellite linkage which would allow an interviewer in Philippi to talk with Paul in Ephesus.

There were two difficulties. One was choosing the best translation or paraphrase for this particular purpose. I chose the American Bible Society's *TEV*, copyright 1966, paraphrase. You might choose one more comfortable to your congregation. The other was finding a reader who could make the biblical material flow smoothly and conversationally for the purpose of the interview.

Paul, The Great Missionary
2 Corinthians 5:16-19

According to recent studies by scholars, it appears that the apostle Paul was put in prison during his ministry in Ephesus. It was during the winter of 54-55 A.D., about a quarter century after the death of Jesus of Nazareth. While in prison, he continued to maintain contact with friends in the churches he helped start. He wrote a number of letters to places all over the eastern end of the Mediterranean Sea, and up into Turkey, a seaport area, across the Aegean Sea, southeast of Philippi, which is in Greece, about 275 miles in distance. The church at Philippi appears to have cared much for Paul and sent a good deal of help.

Imprisonment wasn't always as rigid as we have it today. Paul's experience seemed more to be like house arrest. His friends could come and go or even stay with him. Most of his expenses were paid for by friends.

Today, we will pretend that we have a radio hookup from Philippi, where Paul's friends in the church are very worried about him, to Ephesus, where Paul is being kept. The words of Paul's replies to the questions can be found in the letter to the Philippians.

We begin:

Announcer: We appreciate the cooperation of the authorities in Philippi who have allowed us this opportunity to talk with our colleague, the missionary, Paul of Tarsus. Many of you, our listeners, have known of him and many more have actually met him, heard him preach, and spent time with him. This is a rare opportunity to be in touch once again.

Paul, do you have any opening remarks you would like to make?

Paul: "I thank my God for you every time I think of you; and every time I pray for you all, I pray with joy, because of the way in which you have helped me in the work of the gospel, from the very first day until now. And so I am sure of this: that God, who began

102

this good work in you, will carry it on until it is finished in the Day of Christ Jesus. You are always in my heart! And so it is only right for me to feel this way about you. For you have shared with me in this privilege that God has given me, both now that I am in prison and also while I was free to defend and firmly establish the gospel. God knows that I tell the truth when I say that my deep feeling for you all comes from the heart of Christ Jesus himself.

"This is my prayer for you: I pray that your love will keep on growing more and more, together with true knowledge and perfect judgment, so that you will be able to choose what is best. Then you will be free from all impurity and blame on the Day of Christ. Your lives will be filled with the truly good qualities which Jesus Christ alone can produce, for the glory and praise of God." (Philippians 1:3-11)

Announcer: It is so good to hear your voice. I'm sure I speak on behalf of all your friends here! We thank you for your concern about us. Now that you are in lockdown, do you think about being set free?

Paul: "I know that by means of your prayers and the help which comes from the Spirit of Jesus Christ, I shall be set free. My deep desire and hope is that I shall be full of courage, so that with my whole being I shall bring honor to Christ, whether I live or die. For what is life? To me it is Christ. Death, then, will bring more. But if by living on I can do more worthwhile work, then I am not sure which I should choose. I am caught from both sides. I want very much to leave this life and be with Christ, which is a far better thing; but it is much more important, for your sake, that I remain alive. I am sure of this, and so I know that I will stay. I will stay on with you all, to add to your progress and joy in the faith. So when I am with you again you will have even more reason to be proud of me, in your life in Christ Jesus." (Philippians 1:19-27)

"Perhaps my life's blood is to be poured out like an offering on the sacrifice that your faith offers to God. If that is so, I am glad, and share my joy with you all. In the same way, you too must be glad and share your joy with me." (Philippians 2:17-18)

Announcer: You do not sound too optimistic about being freed. We admire your ability to look at what is happening to you and yet you still find a way to be positive. In the midst of the strain of imprisonment, what holds you together?

Paul: "Does your life in Christ make you strong? Does his love comfort you? Do you have fellowship with the Spirit? Do you feel kindness and compassion for one another? I urge you, then, make me completely happy by having the same thoughts, sharing the same love, and being one in soul and body. Don't do anything from selfish ambition, or from a cheap desire to boast; but be humble toward each other, never thinking you are better than others. And look out for each other's interests, not just for your own. The attitude you should have is the one Christ Jesus had:

He always had the very nature of God, but he did not think that by force he should try to become equal with God.

Instead, of his own free will, he gave it all up, and took the nature of a servant.

He became like man, and appeared in human likeness.

He was humble and walked the path of obedience to death — his death upon the cross.

For this reason God raised him to the highest place above, and gave him the name that is greater than any other name.

And so, in honor of the name of Jesus, all beings in heaven, on earth, and in the world below will fall on their knees,

and all will openly proclaim that Jesus Christ is the Lord, to the glory of God the Father." (Philippians 2:1-11)

Announcer: We ask you what holds you together and you ask us what holds us together! Some of our listeners recognized that poem you recited and said it along with you. I guess we feel held together by our faith in Christ much the same way. You were our preacher, right? Can you tell us how you feel about your captors?

Paul: "I want you to know, my brothers and sisters, that the things that have happened to me have really helped the progress of the gospel. As a result, the whole palace guard and all the others here know that I am in prison because I am a servant of Christ." (Philippians 1:12-13)

"Don't be afraid of your enemies; always be courageous, and this will prove to them that they will lose, and that you will win, because it is God who gives you the victory." (Philippians 1:28)

Announcer: It is hard not to be intimidated by soldiers and weapons. But we will try. Some of us watched you as a runner in some of the games years ago and remember how you often beat some bigger and stronger racers, just by being so gutsy when they shoved you around. You speak with authority, my friend. Speaking of friends, how are your friends there in the Ephesus church taking the imprisonment?

Paul: "My being in prison has given most of the brothers and sisters more confidence in the Lord, so that they grow bolder all the time in preaching the message without fear. Of course, some of them preach Christ because they are jealous and quarrelsome, but others preach him with all good will. These do so from love, because they know that God has given me the work of defending the gospel. The others do not proclaim Christ sincerely, but from a spirit of selfish ambition; they think that they will make more trouble for me while I'm in prison. It does not matter! I am happy about it — just so Christ is preached in every way possible, whether from right or wrong motives." (Philippians 1:14-18)

Announcer: Did the things we sent get through to you?

Paul: "It was very good of you to help me in my troubles. You Philippians yourselves know very well that when I left Macedonia, in the early days of preaching the Good News, you were the only church to help me; you were the only one who shared my profits and losses. More than once, when I needed help in Thessalonica, you sent it to me. It is not that I just want to receive gifts; rather I want to see profit added to your account. Here, then, is my receipt for everything you have given me — and it has been more than enough! I have all I need, now that Epaphroditus has brought me all your gifts. These are like a sweet-smelling offering to God, a sacrifice which is acceptable and pleasing to him." (Philippians 4:14-18)

Announcer: If you have to stay imprisoned much longer, please let us know and we will do what more we can. We have been lucky to get this hookup. Can you tell us how you will be getting your messages out after this?

Paul: "I trust in the Lord that I will be able to send Timothy out to you soon, so that I may be encouraged by news of you. He is the only one who shares my feelings, and who really cares about you. Everyone else is concerned only about his or her own affairs, not about the cause of Jesus Christ. And you yourselves know how he has proved his worth, how he and I, like a man and his father, have worked together for the sake of the gospel. I hope to send him to you then, as soon as I know how things are going to turn out for me. And I trust in the Lord that I myself will be able to come to you soon.

"I have thought it necessary to send you our brother Epaphroditus, who had worked and fought by my side, and who has served as your messenger in helping me. He is anxious to see you all, and is very upset because you heard that he was sick. Indeed he was sick, and almost died. But God had pity on him, and not only on him but on me, too, and spared me even greater sorrow. I am all the more eager, then, to send him to you, so that you will be glad again when you see him, and my own sorrow will disappear. Receive him, then, with all joy, as a brother in the Lord. Show respect to all such men as he, because he risked his life and nearly died, for the sake of the work of Christ, in order to give me the help that you yourselves could not give." (Philippians 2:19-30)

Announcer: Thank you for the news about our friend, Epaphroditus. We had received only rumors and were very worried. We will be happy to receive him back with us. We are sorry his illness caused you so much anguish. You must be going through a lot there. What has been your greatest concern while you've been in prison?

Paul: "All I want is to know Christ and to experience the power of his resurrection; to share in his sufferings and become more like him in his death, in the hope that I myself will be raised from death to life.

"I do not claim that I have already succeeded or have already become perfect. I keep going on to try to win the prize for which Christ Jesus has already won me to himself. Of course, my brothers and sisters, I do not think that I have already won it; the only thing I do, however, is to forget what is behind me and do my best to reach what is ahead. So I run straight toward the goal in order to win the prize, which is God's call through Christ Jesus to the life above.

106

"All of us who are spiritually mature should have this same attitude. If, however, some of you have a different attitude, God will make this clear to you. However that may be, let us go forward according to the same rules we have followed until now.

"Keep on imitating me, my brothers and sisters. We have set the right example for you, so pay attention to those who follow it." (Philippians 3:10-17)

Announcer: So we will, our elder brother and friend. Any more orders for us to consider?

Paul: "Dear friends, as you always obeyed me when I was with you, it is even more important that you obey me now, while I am away from you. Keep on working, with fear and trembling, to complete your salvation, because God is always at work in you to make you willing and able to obey his own purpose.

"Do everything without complaining or arguing, so that you may be innocent and pure, as God's perfect children who live in a world of corrupt and sinful people. You must shine among them like stars lighting up the sky, as you offer them the message of life. If you do so, I shall have reason to be proud of you on the Day of Christ, because it will show that all my effort has not been wasted." (Philippians 2:12-16)

"So then, my brothers and sisters — and how dear you are to me, and how I miss you! How happy you make me, and how proud I am of you — this, dear brothers and sisters, is how you should stand firm in your life in the Lord.

"Euodia and Syntyche, please, I beg you, try to agree as sisters in the Lord. And you, too, my faithful partner, I want you to help these women; for they have worked hard with me to spread the gospel, together with Clement and all my other fellow workers, whose names are in God's book of the living.

"May you always be joyful in your life in the Lord. I say it again: rejoice!

"Show a gentle attitude toward all. The Lord is coming soon. Don't worry about anything, but in all your prayers ask God for what you need, always asking him with a thankful heart. And God's peace, which is far beyond human understanding, will keep your hearts and minds safe, in union with Christ Jesus.

"In conclusion, my brothers and sisters, fill your minds with those things that are good and deserve praise: things that are true, noble, right, pure, lovely, and honorable. Put into practice what you learned and received from me, both from my words and from my deeds. And the God who gives us peace will be with you." (Philippians 4:1-9)

Announcer: We are grateful to authorities both here and in Ephesus for allowing us to have this conversation with you. We have heard your admonitions. I will do what I can to help reconcile our friends, and it will be far easier to keep a positive attitude after having this chance to talk with you again.

Paul, our dear friend, may the peace of God be with you always.

www.ingramcontent.com/pod-product-compliance
Lightning Source LLC
LaVergne TN
LVHW051658080426
835511LV00017B/2626